Bloom's Modern Critical Interpretations

Adventures of
    Huckleberry Finn
All Quiet on the
    Western Front
Animal Farm
Beloved
Beowulf
Billy Budd, Benito
    Cereno, Bartleby
    the Scrivener, and
    Other Tales
The Bluest Eye
Brave New World
Cat on a Hot Tin Roof
The Catcher in the Rye
Catch-22
Cat's Cradle
The Color Purple
Crime and Punishment
The Crucible
Daisy Miller, The
    Turn of the Screw,
    and Other Tales
David Copperfield
Death of a Salesman
The Divine Comedy
Don Quixote
Dracula
Dubliners
Emma
Fahrenheit 451
A Farewell to Arms
Frankenstein
The General Prologue
    to the Canterbury
    Tales
The Glass Menagerie
The Grapes of Wrath
Great Expectations
The Great Gatsby
Gulliver's Travels

Hamlet
The Handmaid's Tale
Heart of Darkness
I Know Why the
    Caged Bird Sings
The Iliad
The Interpretation of
    Dreams
Invisible Man
Jane Eyre
The Joy Luck Club
Julius Caesar
The Jungle
King Lear
Long Day's Journey
    Into Night
Lord of the Flies
The Lord of the Rings
Macbeth
The Merchant of Venice
The Metamorphosis
A Midsummer Night's
    Dream
Moby-Dick
My Ántonia
Native Son
Night
1984
The Odyssey
Oedipus Rex
The Old Man and
    the Sea
One Flew Over the
    Cuckoo's Nest
One Hundred Years
    of Solitude
Othello
Paradise Lost
The Pardoner's Tale
A Portrait of the Artist
    as a Young Man

Pride and Prejudice
Ragtime
The Red Badge
    of Courage
The Rime of the
    Ancient Mariner
Romeo & Juliet
The Scarlet Letter
A Scholarly Look at
    The Diary of
    Anne Frank
A Separate Peace
Silas Marner
Slaughterhouse-Five
Song of Myself
Song of Solomon
The Sonnets of
    William Shakespeare
Sophie's Choice
The Sound and
    the Fury
The Stranger
A Streetcar Named
    Desire
Sula
The Sun Also Rises
A Tale of Two Cities
The Tales of Poe
The Tempest
Tess of the
    D'Urbervilles
Their Eyes Were
    Watching God
Things Fall Apart
To Kill a Mockingbird
Waiting for Godot
Walden
The Waste Land
White Noise
Wuthering Heights

Modern Critical Interpretations

Harper Lee's
TO KILL A MOCKINGBIRD

Edited and with an introduction by
Harold Bloom
Sterling Professor of the Humanities
Yale University

CHELSEA HOUSE PUBLISHERS
Philadelphia

© 1999 by Chelsea House Publishers,
a subsidiary of Haights Cross Communications.

Introduction © 1999 by Harold Bloom

All rights reserved. No part of this publication may be
reproduced or transmitted in any form or by any means
without the written permission of the publisher.

Printed and bound in the United States of America

10 9 8 7 6 5

∞ The paper used in this publication meets the minimum
requirements of the American National Standard for Perma-
nence of Paper for Printed Library Materials,
Z39.48-1984

Library of Congress Cataloging-in-Publication Data

To kill a mockingbird / edited and with an introduction by
Harold Bloom.
        p. 150 cm. — (Modern critical interpretations)
    Includes bibliographical references and index.
    ISBN 0-7910-4779-2 (hardcover)
    1. Lee, Harper.   To kill a mockingbird.   I. Bloom,
Harold.   II. Series.
PS3562.E353T6335   1998
813'.54—dc21   98-23258
                                            CIP

Contents

Editor's Note   vii

Introduction   1
  Harold Bloom

Children Play; Adults Betray   3
  Harding LeMay

Three at the Outset   5
  Granville Hicks

Discovering Theme and Structure in
the Novel   7
  Edgar H. Schuster

Keen Scalpel on Racial Ills   17
  Edwin Bruell

A Censorship Attempt in Hanover, Virginia, 1966   23
  edited by *Claudia Durst Johnson*

The Romantic Regionalism of Harper Lee   39
  Fred Erisman

To Kill a Mockingbird: Harper Lee's Tragic Vision   49
  R.A. Dave

Store and Mockingbird: Two Pulitzer Novels
about Alabama   61
  William T. Going

The Secret Courts of Men's Hearts: Code and
Law in Harper Lee's *To Kill a Mockingbird*   67
    Claudia Durst Johnson

Literary Analysis: Unifying Elements of
To Kill a Mockingbird   79
    Claudia Durst Johnson

Hollywood and Race: *To Kill a Mockingbird*   89
    Colin Nicholson

Atticus Finch and the Mad Dog:
Harper Lee's *To Kill a Mockingbird*   99
    Carolyn Jones

The Female Voice in *To Kill a Mockingbird*:
Narrative Strategies in Film and the Novel   115
    Dean Shackelford

Chronology   127

Contributors   129

Bibliography   131

Acknowledgments   133

Index   135

Editor's Note

This volume gathers together a representative collection of critical essays that interpret Harper Lee's very popular novel, *To Kill a Mockingbird*. The essays are reprinted in the chronological order of their original publication.

My Introduction asks, but does not answer, the question as to aesthetic value: is *To Kill a Mockingbird* a permanent work or a period piece (1960), reflecting its particular moment in American cultural history?

The chronological sequence of essays begins with Harding LeMay, who doubts that the novel adequately fuses its personal and social scenes, and with a note by Granville Hicks, who doubts Harper Lee's consistency in staying within the limits of Scout Finch's mind.

Edgar H. Schuster centers upon classroom techniques for discussing Lee's novel, while Edwin Bruell contrasts *Mockingbird* with Alan Paton's South African narrative, *Cry, the Beloved Country*.

Claudia Durst Johnson, the leading authority on Harper Lee, details one of the many attempts to censor *Mockingbird*, after which Fred Erisman argues that Lee presents "an Emersonian view of Southern Romanticism."

R. A. Dave finds tragic elements in the book, while William T. Going brings together the book's twin obsessions with childhood and the law. Two essays by Claudia Durst Johnson follow, the first on the tension between "code and law" in *Mockingbird*, and the second arguing forcibly that the novel is highly unified.

Colin Nicholson finds equivocal the moral resolutions both of Lee's book, and the film based upon it, after which Carolyn Jones reaches an opposite conclusion, centering on the ethical strength of Atticus Finch.

The novel and the film are again contrasted by Dean Shackelford, who finds more of a feminist emphasis in the book than in Horton Foote's screen adaptation.

Introduction

I find that rereading *To Kill a Mockingbird* (wonderful title!) is, for me, a somewhat ambivalent experience. Scout Finch charms me, as she has so many millions of people, and yet she seems to me better than her book, which has dated into a period piece, while she herself remains remarkably vital and refreshing. Since Scout *is* her book, I find my own reaction an enigma, and hope to enlighten at least myself in this "Introduction." No one could expect Scout to rival Huck Finn (from whom she serenely derives), and yet her sensibility, intelligence, and decency strongly recall aspects of Huck. This, I think, is all to the good: a younger, female Huckleberry Finn fills a void in American fiction. The aesthetic problem is not Scout Finch, but her father, Atticus, and the entire range of major and minor characters in the story. Atticus and all the others are ideograms rather than people, while Harper Lee's portrait of the artist as a young girl has the individuality, of consciousness and of speech, that allows the representation of a person to be much more than a name on a page.

Harper Lee cannot sustain comparison with Eudora Welty and Flannery O'Connor, or even with Carson McCullers. It would be wrong to make such a contrast, except that to see the limits of *To Kill a Mockingbird* is also to perceive better the novel's relative success in portraying Scout Finch. It is very difficult to represent any healthy consciousness in literature, whether we are being shown an eight-year-old girl or a fully mature woman. Shakespeare, most prodigious of all writers ever, has an astonishing triumph in the Rosalind of *As You Like It*, a heroine who is not only a superb wit, like Falstaff and Hamlet, but who manifests an absolutely normative consciousness, free of all neuroses and darknesses. As an audience, we cannot achieve any perspectives upon Rosalind in which she has not preceded us. She sees all around, as it were, and has a largeness that inspired Jane Austen to emulation. A wholesome sensibility attracts us in life, yet rarely confronts us in literature. One cannot expect Scout Finch to grow up into Rosalind; Scout

1

is perceptive and quick, but her mind is essentially conventional. And yet her spirit is free, in a kind of proto-feminist variation upon Huck Finn's.

The story that Scout tells is circumscribed by time and by region, and also by an America before the Fall, in our final Age of Innocence, the Fifties. Harper Lee and her book emerged from a country yet to experience the Vietnamese War, and the subsequent advent of the Counterculture. The United States, as it hazards the last years before the Millennium, is a nation desperately losing faith in all authority, whether governmental or familial. *To Kill a Mockingbird*, in its societal aspects, is already a period piece, and its faith in essential human nature can seem very naive. The book's continued popularity, still extraordinary, partly suggests that we find in it a study of the nostalgias. Yet nostalgia itself dates; the reader becomes alienated from it, when nothing restores a sense of its relevance. There remains the portrait of Scout Finch. Her voice, for now, retains immediacy, and speaks for and to many among us. Whether she will survive the aspects of her story that time has staled, I cannot prophesy.

HARDING LEMAY

Children Play; Adults Betray

In her first novel, *To Kill a Mockingbird*, Harper Lee makes a valiant attempt to combine two dominant themes of contemporary Southern fiction—the recollection of childhood among village eccentrics and the spirit-corroding shame of the civilized white Southerner in the treatment of the Negro. If her attempt fails to produce a novel of stature, or even of original insight, it does provide an exercise in easy, graceful writing and some genuinely moving and mildly humorous excursions into the transient world of childhood.

Set during the depression, the story is recalled from the distance of maturity by Jean Louise ("Scout") Finch, whose widowed father, Atticus, was a civilized, tolerant lawyer in a backward Alabama town. An older brother, Jem, and a summer visitor from Mississippi, Dill, share Scout's adventures and speculations among figures not totally unfamiliar to readers of Carson McCullers, Eudora Welty, and Truman Capote. . . . [The children] play their games of test and dare with ill-tempered old ladies, buzzing village gossips, and, most especially, with the mysterious occupant of the house next door who has never been seen outside since his father locked him up over fifteen years earlier. It is through Boo Radley whose invisible presence tantalizes the children, that Miss Lee builds the most effective part of her novel: an exploration of the caution and curiosity between which active children expend their energies and imaginations.

From *New York Herald Tribune Book Review*, July 10, 1960. © 1960 by Harding LeMay.

In the second half of the novel, Atticus defends a Negro accused of raping a white girl. The children add to their more innocent games that of watching a Southern court in action. They bring to the complexities of legal argument the same luminous faith in justice that sweeps through their games, and they watch, with dismay and pain, as the adult world betrays them. And here, perhaps because we have not been sufficiently prepared for the darkness and the shadows, the book loses strength and seems contrived. For everything happens as we might expect. The children are stained with terror and the knowledge of unreasoning hatreds but gain in insight and in compassion, and the author, deliberately using Atticus and an elderly widow as mouthpieces, makes her points about the place of civilized man in the modern South.

The two themes Miss Lee interweaves throughout the novel emerge as enemies of each other. The charm and wistful humor of the childhood recollections do not foreshadow the deeper, harsher note which pervades the later pages of the book. The Negro, the poor white girl who victimizes him, and the wretched community spirit that defeats him, never rise in definition to match the eccentric, vagrant, and appealing characters with which the story opens. The two worlds remain solitary in spite of Miss Lee's grace of writing and honorable decency of intent.

GRANVILLE HICKS

Three at the Outset

Harper Lee's *To Kill a Mockingbird* gives a friendly but for the most part unsentimental account of life in an Alabama town in the 1930s. The narrator, Jean Louise (commonly called Scout) Finch, is writing of a time when she was seven or eight years old, and the book is in part the record of a childhood. Their mother being dead, Scout and her brother Jem have been brought up by their father, a lawyer and legislator, and by a Negro servant, Calpurnia. The father, Atticus Finch, is an unusual man, and their childhood is in many ways a unique one.

Miss Lee, however, is not primarily concerned with childhood experience; she has, in her own way, written a novel about the perennial Southern problem. Atticus is assigned to defend a Negro charged with raping a white woman, and, to the dismay of his neighbors, he really tries to defend him. Through Scout's eyes we watch the growth of resentment in the community and then we see the trial itself, in which Atticus is inevitably defeated. After that there is a melodramatic conclusion.

Miss Lee's problem has been to tell the story she wants to tell and yet to stay within the consciousness of a child, and she hasn't consistently solved it. Some episodes in the trial and the melodramatic conclusion seem contrived. But her insight into Southern mores is impressive, and in Atticus she has done a notable portrait of a Southern liberal.

From *Saturday Review* XLIII:30 (July 23, 1960). © 1960 by Granville Hicks.

EDGAR H. SCHUSTER

Discovering *Theme and Structure in the Novel*

> In English, I feel that we will progress only when we see that the ultimately important things to teach boys and girls are the processes of examination of language and literature rather than a sequence of factual conclusions arrived at by others who have examined them.

So spoke G. Robert Carlsen in his 1962 Presidential Address at the NCTE Convention in Florida. It is my intention here to describe a "process of examination" by which boys and girls may be helped to see some important features of theme and structure in novels. The particular novel which I have chosen to illustrate the process is Harper Lee's *To Kill a Mockingbird*, a book that has ranked second in popularity only to *The Catcher in the Rye* among my students during the past two years.

Students enjoy reading *To Kill a Mockingbird*, but my experience has been that their appreciation is meager. Over and over again their interpretations stress the race prejudice issue to the exclusion of virtually everything else. For them, the key moments are the trial scene and the death of Tom Robinson. Consequently, the first part of the book and the last five chapters usually "drag." It seems to me that any interpretation that regards the whole first half of a novel merely as prologue and the last tenth as epilogue is in dire

From *English Journal* 52:7 (1963). © 1963 by the National Council of Teachers of English.

need of refinement. By what process of examination may one encourage a finer critical appraisal, a richer and deeper appreciation?

In the pages that follow I shall set forth both a practical classroom approach to the novel and an interpretation of *To Kill a Mockingbird* based on that approach. The reader should bear in mind that I am dealing here primarily with the elements of theme and structure. A fuller treatment of the novel would undoubtedly settle on a number of issues relating to plot and character, two aspects of the novel that I have slighted in this article.

The Importance of Scale

It is not difficult to teach students the distinction between full and summary rendering. Furthermore, through their work in composition they are already familiar with the principle that the more space one gives an incident or idea, the more emphasis it receives. In fiction, it follows that those incidents that are fully rendered and those that are relatively long will be keys to the author's intention. After students have read the novel, they can be asked to make a catalog of the lengthy and fully rendered episodes as a prelude to the discovery of its full meaning.

In the first half of *Mockingbird* this process of examination will reveal that the Radley house and its phantom occupant play a major part. Fully rendered episodes concerning Radley occur in Chapter 1 and in Chapters 4 through 7. Chapter 8, dealing with the fire at Miss Maudie's, also contains an important reference to Boo Radley. Other major, fully rendered scenes in Part I focus on Scout's classroom, on Atticus' shooting of the mad dog, and on Mrs. Dubose. Interestingly enough, only in Chapter 9 is any significant reference made to the race prejudice issue, the issue that plays such a large part in the second half of the book and in the typical student interpretation of the novel.

In that second half, the trial scene is indeed important. It is rendered in great detail and it consumes roughly fifteen percent of the total length of the novel. It is not, however, the only extended full rendering in Part II. The last scene—beginning in Chapter 28 and continuing to the end of the novel—is rendered in great detail. Except for the fact that some of it deals with how Ewell gets his "comeupance," it has little or nothing to do with the race prejudice issue.

Once the students have completed their catalog, the teacher might ask a leading question: If *Mockingbird* is primarily a race relations novel, why is it that the author gives such a full treatment to episodes that seem totally unrelated to this theme?

Thematic Motifs

Another process of examination has to do with the discovery and tracing of thematic motifs. In my experience students are too ready to look for the theme of a book before they have found the themes.

The work of tracing the thematic motifs through the novel is perhaps best done in small groups, each group being assigned a specific motif, which its members follow through an assigned number of chapters. The group can then put their work together and determine what generalizations can be made about their theme. Finally, they can share their results with the rest of the class through brief oral reports.

My students and I have identified five thematic motifs in *To Kill a Mockingbird*. Space will permit me to discuss only two of these at any length, but I shall name the other three as well.

One of the motifs—largely understated due to the novel's point of view—concerns Jem's physiological and psychological growth. Although this growth motif may have more to do with character than with theme, the two elements are ultimately bound; moreover it seems clear that the growth of Jem (and of his sister as well) is intimately related to the theme and structure of the novel.

A second thematic motif is centered around what Miss Lee calls the "caste system" in Maycomb. This motif—brought up in many places throughout the book—is obviously related to other motifs, such as growth, superstition, and education. Furthermore, it is within the context of the "caste system" motif that Aunt Alexandria's "missionary circle" and all their talk about the Mrunas and J. Grimes Everett is to be understood.

Thirdly, the title of a novel, students should know, often points to one of its key themes, and this is obviously the case in *To Kill a Mockingbird*. Mockingbirds are mentioned in several places throughout the book, often in key scenes. Best of all, the tracing of this motif will reveal clearly to the students that Tom Robinson is not the only "mockingbird" in the novel.

Finally, the thematic motifs that I would like to discuss in fuller detail are those dealing with *education* and *superstition*. The education motif comes up early in the novel and persists until very near the end. On a number of occasions we are taken into Scout's classroom where we are exposed to the "Dewey Decimal System" in operation. At first glance it is easy for an educator to regard the "anti-progressive" comments of the author as personal animosity. Reflection will reveal, however, that the education motif—far from being incidental—is a center for the ironic contrast between what is "taught" and what is "learned," a contrast that lies at the very heart of the novel.

In the course of their growing up the children do a great deal of learning, but little of that learning takes place in school. Jem and Scout learn from experience; their teachers are not Miss Caroline and Miss Gates, but Atticus, Calpurnia, and Alexandria. Their most effective "teacher," however, is life itself, their experience. Ironically, they learn "by doing," precisely what Dewey would have wanted.

It is not Dewey's approach that is being criticized, then, but its implementation. The learn by doing approach, Miss Lee implies, is dependent upon the teacher. What can Miss Caroline teach about getting along with others when she herself knows virtually nothing about the human beings she is instructing? And what can Scout learn about democracy in action from Miss Gates, who worries about Negroes "getting above themselves" and marrying whites?

Scout makes her final ironic comment on classroom education in the last chapter. She is in the third grade when she says, ". . . I thought Jem and I would get grown but there wasn't much else left for us to learn, except possibly algebra."

Superstition is another key motif running through the novel. Superstitions are, of course, the product of fear and ignorance. We expect them to disappear as fear and ignorance are replaced by security and knowledge, and this is clearly what happens, at least to the children, as the novel progresses.

The most memorable superstition in the book is the one concerning the "hot places." Because of its uniqueness, it stands as a kind of symbol of superstition in general. It is first introduced in Chapter 4 in a conversation between the Finch children and Dill; the last reference to it occurs in Chapter 28, when Jem and Scout are passing in front of the Radley Place. They do not run by as they used to, and Jem asks Scout whether she is "scared of haints."

> We laughed. Haints, Hot Steams, incantations, secret signs, had vanished with our years as mist with sunrise. "What was that old thing," Jem said, "Angel right, life-in-death; get off the road, don't suck my breath."

The reader may wonder why I have ignored race prejudice in my handling of the thematic motifs of the novel. My reasons for this are two. First of all, I am not sure that race prejudice is a *motif*; it tends to be concentrated in one section of the novel rather than to be spread throughout the book as the other motifs are. Secondly, the children—raised by Atticus and Calpurnia—are almost completely free of such prejudice; they certainly feel no antagonism toward Tom Robinson.

On the other hand, no one would deny that *Mockingbird* deals with race prejudice. The point here is to attempt to discover how it fits into the total pattern of the novel. I prefer to hold off this problem till the final section of my article.

Emphatic Positions

Every high school student knows (or *should* know) that the emphatic positions in a piece of writing are the first and the last. Thus in a novel the first and last chapter and the chapters at the beginning and the end of the sections of the novel (Chapters 11 and 12 in *Mockingbird*) would be of special importance. An intensive investigation might carry this further by focusing some attention on the beginning and end of each chapter.

I would suggest that the teacher approach the matter of emphatic positions by asking his students to reread the relevant chapters (1, 11, 12, and 31 in *Mockingbird*), making notes on the points that are treated in them with special attention to the following: (1) the beginning and end of the relevant chapters, (2) the relationships among these chapters with respect to repetitions of all sorts, and (3) the ways in which the final chapter serves as a fulfillment of the earlier ones.

It is always a good practice for students to reread at least the first chapter of a novel after they have finished the whole book (except perhaps in those cases in which the first chapter serves only as introduction). This practice yields especially good results with *To Kill a Mockingbird*, but for the moment, I would like to discuss only Chapters 1, 11, and 12.

The novel opens with the reference to Jem's bad arm and the argument between the children over who started it all. Scout blames it on the Ewells, but Jem claims that it began when Dill first came and gave them the idea of making Boo Radley come out. Although Atticus says that both children are right, the author tacitly confirms Jem's view by devoting her first fully rendered scene to the meeting with Dill and Jem's "foray" on the Radley Place.

It is also in this chapter that Dill wagers his copy of *The Gray Ghost* against two Tom Swifts that Jem won't touch Radley's house. Here, too, we learn of the "summertime boundaries" of the children—the Dubose house two doors to the north and the Radley Place three doors to the south. Mrs. Dubose is "gray" in age; Radley lives in a "gray house." Both characters are "ghosts" in the sense that the children do not know them; fear and prejudice and superstition surround both homes. All these facts should be kept in mind as the novel moves toward fulfillment.

The fact that Miss Lee chose to make more than a Chapter division between Chapters 11 and 12 suggests that she wished to make Chapter 11 more emphatic than it would otherwise have been. We must assume this chapter to be of critical importance in the novel.

Chapter 11 deals with Mrs. Dubose, whose home is the northern boundary of the children's world. In the chapter the children learn what she is really like, that she is not the ghost or ghoul they had made her out to be. At the end of the chapter Mrs. Dubose sends Jem a camellia in a candy box. He throws the box into the fire, but resists the temptation to destroy the flower as well. (The fact that the box is a *candy* box is a small but interesting detail.) The gist of the episode is that Jem is growing up, learning about life through experience.

Any reader who is skeptical of the importance of this point need only turn the page. Chapter 12 begins with the sentence, "Jem was twelve," and goes on to underscore his growing maturity when Calpurnia calls him *Mister* Jem. The growth, of course, is more than physical, and the juxtaposition of Chapter 11 with the opening of Chapter 12 should leave no doubt in the reader's mind of the importance of the Dubose episode.

Chapter 12 contains other items of interest. It is here that Scout and Jem visit the Negro church, where reference is made to Tom Robinson, and the race prejudice issue begins to assume importance. The most emphatic section of the chapter, however, its end, concludes as follows:

> We were on the sidewalk by the Radley Place.
> "Look on the porch yonder," Jem said.
> I looked over to the Radley Place, expecting to see its phantom occupant sunning himself in the swing. The swing was empty.
> "I mean our porch," said Jem.
> I looked down the street. Enarmored, upright, uncompromising, Aunt Alexandria was sitting in a rocking chair exactly as if she had sat there every day of her life.

The northern boundary of the children's world has become known and has played its role in the maturing of Jem. In the above passage we are reminded that the southern boundary, however, (the knowing of which will be a main element in the growth of Scout) is still unknown. By implication we also learn that Aunt Alexandria is to be an important stimulus in the same direction.

The method of approach that I have been discussing assumes that the students have read the novel. Much the same plan can be followed, however, by asking the students to keep a notebook while they read. The notebook would contain the headings—scale, thematic motifs, and emphasis—and the students would enter their observations under each of these headings. The only change that would have to be made would be that the teacher would alert the students to the thematic motifs and perhaps to the first instance of each. The students might also be asked to reread each of the emphatic chapters.

Intention and Interpretation

Before continuing to my final conclusions I would like to deal briefly with two vexing questions that inevitably arise in any classroom discussion of the meaning and interpretation of a literary work.

The first of these questions is, "How do you know that the author really intended 'meaning A'?" One of the best answers to this question is "How do you know that he didn't?" This reply is not intended to put an end to the discussion; rather it should serve as a prelude to a treatment of the whole matter of intention in fiction.

If meaning A, say, is rejected, its rejection implies that some other meaning—B or C or D—is a more adequate description of the facts. Upon what grounds does one dismiss one meaning or interpretation and accept another? Students are apt to say that the "correct" interpretation is the one the author intended. In most cases, however, we do not possess a statement of intention from the author. Furthermore, even if we did, we could not guarantee that it would be a dependable guide. Any student who has done some writing on his own should be aware that powerful unconscious forces affect the creative process.

All this adds up to the assumption that the best way of discovering intention is to consult the book rather than the author. A careful study of scale, thematic motifs, positions of emphasis, and structure will provide the most dependable key to intention and meaning. If the book is badly done, we may not learn what the author consciously intended, but we will learn what he has in fact communicated.

The second vexing question concerns the validity of interpretations. "Isn't it true," some student inevitably asks, "that any interpretation is as good as any other? " The answer to this question must be negative, for to answer affirmatively is to open the door to complacency. If any interpretation is as good as any other, why bother to think? What is to prevent me from projecting my own set of problems and solutions on to every book I read? A student ought to *yield himself to a book*. He is not likely to do so if he carries with him the complacent notion that any interpretation is as good as any other.

Of course it is not difficult to dispel this misconception. As soon as one speaks of "good" and "bad" interpretations, he is discussing values, obviously. And it is equally obvious that the validation of value judgments requires standards. The classroom teacher must encourage students to become conscious of the standards that underlie such judgments.

Structure and the Final Synthesis

After the class has discussed intention and standards by which interpretations can be validated, they should be prepared to consider the novel's structure. This discussion should ideally be based upon all the elements previously examined. As a prelude to a full class discussion, the students might be asked to write their own interpretations. Another possibility is for the teacher to suggest several interpretations which the students could criticize on the basis of what they have learned through their analysis of scale, thematic motifs, and emphatic positions.

The standards for validating interpretations will perhaps vary somewhat in their minor details, but among the more universal standards it seems to me that we must include *exhaustiveness*; that is to say, a good interpretation should explain the *whole* book. (Logical consistency and simplicity are two other standards that my classes invariably use, but I do not have space here to discuss them.)

An exhaustive interpretation is best arrived at through a consideration of the novel's structure, that is, the overall design of the work. Assuming that the novel possesses unity, its structure will serve as a matrix into which all thematic motifs as well as all major incidents and characters will fit.

A discovery of the structure of *To Kill a Mockingbird* must begin by focusing on the first chapter: the summertime boundaries, the "gray ghosts," the tension centered in the question of what Boo Radley is really like. How do these phenomena fit into the over-all design?

If that design is to be truly "over-all," it is obvious that the final chapter, too, must play a key role. It is in this chapter—just after having escorted the real Boo Radley home—that Scout makes the point about growing up and algebra; it is here that she says that one never knows a man unless he stands in his shoes and walks around in them; here that she realizes that "nothin's real scary except in books"; and here, finally, that Atticus reads to her from *The Gray Ghost*. The novel concludes with Scout revealing some of the content of that book:

"An' they chased him 'n' never could catch him 'cause they didn't know what he looked like, an' Atticus, when they finally saw him, why he hadn't done any of those things . . . Atticus, he was real nice. . . . "

His hands were under my chin, pulling up the cover, tucking it around me.

"Most people are, Scout, when you finally see them."

And so the gray ghosts—Dubose and Radley in particular—and superstitions and prejudices of *all* kinds are gone, banished by security and knowledge—the security stemming from the love and example of Atticus, the knowledge coming from real contact with real people.

The achievement of Harper Lee is not that she has written another novel about race prejudice, but rather that she has placed race prejudice in a perspective which allows us to see it as an aspect of a larger thing; as something that arises from phantom contacts, from fear and lack of knowledge; and finally as something that disappears with the kind of knowledge or "education" that one gains through learning what people are really like when you "finally see them." Students who have studied the novel through the process of examination that I have outlined have successfully perceived many of the elements of the final synthesis that has just been suggested; indeed, my students have contributed almost as much to this synthesis as I have. Examinations of other novels based on a study of the elements of scale, thematic motifs, positions of emphasis, and structure are bound to be fruitful. What is more, they are certain to make students much more broadly and deeply conscious of the aspects of theme and structure than they normally are.

EDWIN BRUELL

Keen Scalpel on Racial Ills

O ne is tempted to make tidy comparisons and sharp contrasts between *Cry, the Beloved Country* and *To Kill a Mockingbird*, novels dealing generally with racial themes, but pat oversimplification is always the danger of those who set out to become scientific and objective about works of art. And works of art these two books are.

Paton has chosen for his setting the brooding continent of Africa, torn by the Boer War and Verwoerd's apartheid and the Afrikaner strife. Despite this full-scale setting with a cyclorama vista, *Cry* is not a panoramic novel, as was Tolstoi's *War and Peace*, or as Margaret Mitchell's *Gone with the Wind* was, almost.

Paton goes inside the heads and hearts of the Reverend Stephen Kumalo and his son Absalom and the sister, Gertrude, the wayward Jezebel who nevertheless had moments of light. There is significance in the son's name, for Absalom was the favorite son of David, who also was killed after rebelling against his father, as this Absalom in rebellion was killed.

Johannesburg, this city of gold, like some modern Sodom or Gomorrah, was partly the villain, or the protagonist of the story. The metropolis represented the restless wandering of the sons and daughters who had left the barren land. Their tribal unity, with its attendant security, had been taken away, and that *something of value*, as Robert Ruark defined it, was

From *English Journal* 53:9 (December 1964). © 1964 by the National Council of Teachers of English.

not given in return. Johannesburg, with its Shantytown and its Kliptown, was much like Chicago's South Side or New York's Harlem. Paton confessedly is influenced by the naturalistic writing of John Steinbeck in *The Grapes of Wrath*, with its primitive Okies who were capable of being fascinated by indoor plumbing. But Paton is no proletarian writer. His novel is rather a lyrical work with Biblical overtones. His words are flowing, and they read well aloud, like all good poetry—much like those of Pearl S. Buck in her masterpiece, *The Good Earth*. Again, however, *Cry* is not an epic novel, for the backdrop of Paton's stage is too close for that.

There are many short speeches, à la Hemingway, without the familiar quotation marks, which the hapless grammarians have decreed. Sometimes we lose the exact tenor of who is talking, but we understand all the same, because always Paton is talking. There is much repetition, which is somehow never offensive: "my brother, my sister, according to the custom, sleep well, go well, heavy—heavily." And always there is the fear, the constant fear. The whole theme is bound up with this ever-present fear: "the fear of bondage and the bondage of fear." All were motivated by fear. Even Absalom, pulling the trigger, was motivated by fear.

Restraint Typifies Novel

There is a surface restraint, with subterranean temblors, in Paton's writing. Consider the scene in which the elder Jarvis faced finally the thought of his son's martyr-like death, when the watcher of the law had observed, shallowly, that "the old chap cannot face it any more." Still the truth was that the elder Jarvis had finally come to understand what his son, who thought differently from his father, really stood for. There was no melodramatic propaganda as in Stowe—no burning intensity as in James Baldwin—no Black Muslim Koran here. There was only the simple phrase from the soon-to-be-martyred son: "Allow me a minute." Then it was done, and a pure man descended to meet the assassin's bullet.

The unseeing townspeople, wanting only quick escape into their giddy whirl of fast-moving pleasure, were much like the townspeople in the *Mockingbird*. With hasty retreat, they tossed over their shoulders the line with the inevitable, pointed, indefinite pronouns: "Why can't they make recreation places for them?"

The author of this paper has his private comments on theme hunting, moral seeking, and symbol chasing in the novel, but Mark Twain said it much better in his preface to his great novel, *The Adventures of Huckleberry Finn*: "Persons attempting to find a motive in this narrative will be prosecuted;

persons attempting to find a moral in it will be banished; persons attempting to find a plot in it will be shot." Alan Paton himself went outside his novel to state the theme when he was eventually feted on Broadway for his work, which was, rather naturally, slow to catch public interest. When Maxwell Anderson's stage adaptation, titled *Lost in the Stars*, was celebrated, Paton said: "It is my own belief that the only power which can resist the power of fear is the power of love."

Within the milieu of a whole society ruled by fear, the judge who sentenced Absalom said, "If the law is the law of a society that some feel to be unjust, it is the law and the society that must be changed." And Paton paraphrases, in his literary contempt of court, "If a law is unjust and the judge judges according to the law, that is justice, even if it is unjust."

Again the theme emerges with a lyric quality when the small boy is dancing with the sustained tremulous cry that echoes when the refrain is chanted: "Yes, God save Africa, the beloved country. God save us from the fear that is afraid of justice." The moving prose herein is like that of the early Sandburg, and it should be read aloud.

About a decade later there came along a book which caused a much more immediate stir, probably because its setting was at our doorstep—in Maycomb, Alabama. This novel is what one might call a wholesome book on an unwholesome theme. Now *wholesome* conjures up visions of *Life with Father, Cheaper by the Dozen, Our Hearts Were Young and Gay, I Remember Mama* and the like, or, perhaps such television fare as "My Three Sons," or "Father Knows Best."

Point of View

Scout is like a prototype of some Girl Scout—worldly-wise occasionally but more at ease in the world bounded by her father's arms. The story is seen through her eyes, though what precocious eyes they sometimes are—like those of the son of the Lady Macduff. Always we see the warm hand of Harper Lee hovering over. Although a committee from an Ivy League university wrote Harper Lee a letter requesting a speech and using the salutation, "Dear Mr. Lee," clearly a blooper was involved, for Miss Lee does write like a woman. She paints Scout in warm tones, and we like the child. She tells the story of the townspeople who were more noticeably stratified than those in *Cry*, and we like what she says.

The alleged transgressor, Tom Robinson, was really an innocent man, who happened to be a Negro. Tom had a withered hand and was motivated more by bewilderment than by fear. As such he was a poor and easy foil for the Erskine Caldwell type of backwoods character, Mayella, who raped easily, and who cried wolf easily. But Mayella was at the same time a lonely character, unfortunate enough to have been brought into an irresponsible, destitute world by a sire like Bob Ewell, who had no noticeable redeeming qualities (the only such character in either novel). Tom was misunderstood and misunderstanding all his life; even in death he was both misunderstood and misunderstanding. He tried futilely to climb the wall of escape, to find his only real escape—sudden death.

Atticus Finch knew the townspeople well, and they were much like any other townspeople except that they happened to live in the South, and they too were afraid—afraid to try to change the system. Atticus said that they were decent folks till they started to deal with the Negro problem. There was Calpurnia, who understood and (there was a twist in this context) tolerated. Like Faulkner's Delsey, "she will endure." There was Miss Carolyn Fisher, who, like too many schoolteachers, knew only the subject she taught—currently.

Miss Lee uses high and telling humor when she depicts the myopic do-gooders of the local missionary circle who alternately squealed and sighed over the remote plight of the Mrunas who were safely distant in the dark continent, the while they stirred up a falsely labeled "Christian" hell for the racially different in their home town. Yes, and there was cutting irony and blanched white sarcasm too when the authoress seemingly reaches the outer limits of her fine sense of tolerance even for the bigoted.

And the town, said Miss Alexandra, strangely, Atticus' sister, was plagued with streaks—"a Drinking Streak, a Gambling Streak, a Mean Streak, a Funny Streak." There was too the caste system, which explained Maycomb's rationalizing perhaps the best of all. Thus, no member of one clan minded his own business. Others were destined to be morbid. Others were predestined to be liars. All members of one clan walked oddly. Others had strange postures, because they were born into strange postures. In short, everyone in town had his or her *place*, and everybody had damned well better keep it.

There was naiveté in Scout and Dill too, when, oppressed by grown-up injustice, Scout talked without knowing, "Let's get a baby." Later they jumped into the same bed, still in pristine innocence, for though this book has satire, it is no modern-day *Tom Jones*.

Novels Are Linked

What is the common ground of the novels by Paton and Harper? It is the twin powers of compassion and understanding. The crotchety Mrs.

Dubose had her reasons for seclusion, and Dolph Raymond had his reasons for the drunken facade, and Editor Underwood had his reasons for his disdain of the Maycomb mind; all these were interwoven with the racial theme.

"To kill a mockingbird" is to kill that which is innocent and harmless—like Tom Robinson. And Atticus—no heroic type but any graceful, restrained, simple person like one from Attica—said in the summing up, "Most people are nice—when you finally see them," ending on a tranquil note. Boo Radley, the shy recluse named Arthur at birth, too, was nice—just different—yes, to use the cliché which even the demagogues mouth, as every human being has a God-given right to be.

The last part of the book was anticlimactic, a little too carefully plotted and cozily put together—even though the avenging furies saw to it that Bob Ewell met the fate he deserved at the hands of Boo Radley and that Tom Robinson's death was partly exonerated.

There were likenesses in the books. The bishop and the schoolmaster and the chief in *Cry* represented the complacent forces of things as they are, like Miss Stephanie and the missionary circle and the schoolmarm in *Mockingbird*. The judges in both were fair; but, unlike those of the *Perry Mason* courtrooms, they rendered unfavorable verdicts. Both were somewhat uncomfortable in the society wherein they lived and aware of its shortcomings, but still they were committed to uphold the law. Both novels showed the superstitions of a folk nature, one through the children and grownups, one through the natives and the Britishers and the Dutch. In both stories we participated in the simple and rich and appealing church services, under poor temporal surroundings.

Further, Jarvis Junior and Senior and Atticus were crusaders on slim chargers, Jarvis Senior spending his money, Jarvis Junior spending his energy and his life, Atticus spending his reputation. All three characters represent the authors' points of view, although Paton obviously does not agree with Jarvis Senior's earlier views before he found the Holy Grail. In both novels the initial truth which schoolteachers eventually learn is manifest—that the motives of children are basically kind and decent until the grown-ups get to them. Observe Jarvis Senior's grandson and Scout and Jem and Dill. Also, both stories show that not all the people are bad, and, what is more, with the exception of Bob Ewell, that the people are not *all* bad. Bird symbols were apparent in both: the titihoya with its forlorn crying; the mockingbird with its blithe singing.

Obviously, both novels concern racial themes, with more distractions, from a sociological point of view, in *Mockingbird*. It must be confessed that this writer's first exposure to this story was in a condensed version, which moved right into the racial theme. Therein lies a plug for avoiding digested masterworks; the gain for the speed reader is too often offset by a loss for the reader in depth.

Differences, too, may be seen. The humor in *Cry* is quite sparse, perhaps best typified by the belated wedding scene, although it is tinged with grimness. In *Cry*, the one whose son was killed went on to forgive. In *Mockingbird*, the one whose daughter was allegedly raped attempted again to murder the human heart. In *Mockingbird*, the defendant was legally innocent and judged guilty by a jury representing the town. In his bewilderment he found a sort of escape—death. In *Cry*, the defendant was legally guilty and judged guilty by society. Because of his fear, though, he pulled the trigger and was hanged.

Cry seems to be a tighter book with less development of a coterie of characters, a device that may be all to the good, for the panoramic novel, in telling too much, may not tell enough for the seeking soul. At the end Paton wonders when the dawn will come: "But when that dawn will come, of our emancipation from the fear of bondage and the bondage of fear, why, that is a secret."

But Harper Lee already *knows* when the dawn will come. At the end she says: "He [Atticus] turned out the light and went into Jem's room. He would be there all night, and he would be there when Jem waked up in the morning."

Edited by
CLAUDIA DURST JOHNSON

A Censorship Attempt in Hanover, Virginia, 1966

This group of documents reflects the history of one very public instance in which *To Kill a Mockingbird* was challenged. The incident began when a prominent physician, W. C. Bosher, the father of a Hanover County student, took a look at the novel his son had brought home to read and decided it was immoral. Dr. Bosher, who was a County Board of Education trustee, was disturbed that his son was reading a book about rape and reported to the school board that the book was "improper for our children to read." On the strength of his motion, the board voted to remove *To Kill a Mockingbird* from the shelves of the Hanover County school libraries.

In the flurry of reportage and exchange of opinions that followed, the board blamed the state, arguing that the County Board had had the novel removed because *To Kill a Mockingbird* had never been on the *state's* list of books approved for state subsidy. When the State Board of Education was challenged about banning the novel, it pointed its finger at the county, saying that the county was free to keep the book on county shelves. The State Board of Education members argued that Harper Lee's novel was not on the approved list solely because no publisher had ever presented *To Kill a Mockingbird* to them for state subsidy. However, it was eventually discovered that thousands of books presented by publishers for places on the approved list had been rejected by the state's censoring board. As in most cases, except for

From *Understanding To Kill a Mockingbird: A Student Casebook to Issues, Sources, and Historic Documents.* © 1994 by Claudia Durst Johnson.

Dr. Bosher's statements to the press, no reason for rejection by county or state was ever given to the public.

The controversy over *To Kill a Mockingbird* is documented in the pages of the Richmond press. Included are news stories reporting the action of the board, editorials, letters to the editor on both sides of the question, and a response from the author, Harper Lee herself. Eventually, the Board backed away from its original decision to take the book out of the library.

Mr. Bumble and the Mockingbird

The Hanover County School Board last night ordered all copies of Harper Lee's novel, *To Kill a Mockingbird*, removed from the county's school library shelves. In the dim vision of the Hanover board, the novel is "immoral literature." It is "improper for our children to read." And so, by unanimous vote, out it goes—and all other books not on the State Board of Education's approved list are to be taken out of circulation also.

As grown-ups who have been out of Hanover County doubtless are aware, *To Kill a Mockingbird* has become a contemporary classic. It is the tender and moving story of a rape trial in Alabama, and of a white lawyer's effort to obtain justice for a Negro client. A more moral novel scarcely could be imagined. The book was a best-seller; it was made into a notable motion picture; it won the Pulitzer Prize for fiction in 1961; it is read by high school students everywhere else in America but in Hanover County, Virginia.

Fortunately, there exists a remedy for this asinine performance by the Hanover board. Let us now turn to the Beadle Bumble Fund. For some years, we have maintained the fund (named for the famous character in *Oliver Twist*, also an immoral novel) with the sole object of redressing the stupidities of public officials.

Mr. Bumble will gladly purchase and mail a paperbacked copy of *To Kill a Mockingbird* to the first 50 students of Lee-Davis High School who write in. The address is Mr. Bumble, The *News-Leader* Forum, 333 East Grace Street, Richmond.

Editorial Page, *Richmond News-Leader*, Wednesday, January 5, 1966, p. 12.

Some Novels' Fate Remains Uncertain
Hanover School Board to Use State List as Guide

"To Kill a Mockingbird" is dead in Hanover County schools, as far as county school officials are concerned, but the fate of such book as "1984," "Catcher in the Rye," and "Grapes of Wrath" remains in doubt.

The Pulitzer Prize–winning book by Harper Lee will not be used in Hanover County schools because in 1960 it was submitted for inclusion on the state aid book list and rejected, said School Board Chairman B. W. Sadler yesterday.

Under a resolution passed by the county school board Tuesday night, all books taken off the state-approved list must be removed from Hanover schools. The resolution also excludes from county schools books that have been rejected for inclusion on the state list, Sadler said.

The three other widely acclaimed novels also were attacked by W. C. Bosher, the Cold Harbor district school board member who initiated the board's actions against "immoral literature."

Son Was Reading

He said the use of "To Kill Mockingbird" at Lee-Davis School had come to his attention when he discovered his son, a junior there, reading the book.

"To Kill a Mockingbird," the story of a rape trial in Alabama and of a white lawyer's attempt to obtain justice for a Negro client, is used as supplemental reading by the English department at Lee-Davis, according to the school's principal, B. V. Aylor.

Bosher labeled George Orwell's "1984," depicting the despotism of a regimented society, a "very seductive and suggestive piece of literature."

The books "1984," "Catcher in the Rye," and "Grapes of Wrath" have never been submitted by publishers for inclusion on the state list. J. D. Salinger's "Catcher in the Rye" is about a prep-school youth. John Steinbeck's "Grapes of Wrath" concerns the poverty of Oklahomans in the 1930s. Steinbeck's book was published in the 1930s; "Catcher in the Rye" and "1984" are post–World War II.

All books not appearing on the state aid list, the school board's resolution says, must be approved by a school faculty committee of not fewer than three members including the principal and librarian, if any, before they may be used at a county school.

"We are not censoring any books," declared Sadler. "We are saying in this instance that since the State Department of Education does have a library committee to review those books that are submitted to them, we would make a mockery of the committee, if we disregard their disapproval of books, he said.

Sadler said the school board's resolution was a general policy statement on the selection of books for county schools and would be turned over to school authorities for execution.

A spokesman for the State Department of Education explained that the list compiled by the state does not necessarily attempt to approve or disapprove of books from a moralistic standpoint.

The list is compiled to advise local school boards of books that the state will subsidize the purchase of, the spokesman said. Last year, 4,521 books were submitted by publishers and 3,361 were placed on the approved list.

Aylor, Lee-Davis principal, said he had received no official notification of the school board's action and that he has not attempted to stop the use of "To Kill a Mockingbird" at the school.

English teachers at the school declined comment on the controversy yesterday, as did Bosher.

At no point in the Tuesday meeting did the board consider a general ban of books not on the state-approved list. But Bosher appeared to express the sentiment of the board when he said "there should be a lot of screening" of the books used in our schools.

Richmond Times-Dispatch, Thursday, January 6, 1966, p. 2.

College Student Defends Morality of Banned Book

Editor, *News-Leader*:

It is with deep regret that I must announce my ineligibility to request a copy of Harper Lee's immoral novel from Mr. Bumble. Unfortunately, I am now a college student and never resided in Hanover County. That is not to say I have not read the book, nor will consider re-reading it at some future date.

As a matter of fact, I can't think of any book I've ever been afraid of.

I recall my high school days very clearly (a very short time ago, critical elders). They were rich with new literary discoveries—many brought to me by a strongly book-minded mother. From the variety of philosophy consistently handed me, I don't believe she ever attempted to do anything more than make me read.

Ah, but parents so often err—for one day she brought me Harper Lee's story (perhaps she didn't realize that it contained the evil word "rape").

What did it do to me? This horrid piece of trash made me laugh and cry a little inside, forced me to live a life that wasn't mine for some hours, actually had the nerve to make me think of problems I had not yet faced.

It was traumatic.

I'm sure it was even immoral . . . if the good people of Hanover say it is.

Only one thing bothers me—why, if the book were so immoral, didn't I ever commit some criminal act as presented in the indecent tale?

People of the northern county, please learn that your brand of conservatism disgusts those of us with minds.

I tell ya, Mr. Bumble, I don't mind some of the citizens of Hanover County, but I sure wouldn't want my sister to marry one.

Alan Markow

"Forum," *Richmond News-Leader,* January 7, 1966, p. 12.

Hiding "Seamy Side" Is False Protection

Members of the Hanover County School Board are absolutely wrong to ban "To Kill a Mockingbird."

"To Kill a Mockingbird," Mr. Salinger's "Catcher in the Rye," and George Orwell's "1984" are sensitive, frightening, awakening, truthful presentations of what could happen and is happening in our life today. Why hide truth from our young people? We need to teach them right from wrong.

We say "Don't," but fail to explain "Why," which is important whenever anyone is corrected or disciplined. We reinforce learning, even in the smallest toddler, as we correct, then accompany it with simple explanations.

Teach them, show them, but let them make choices whenever possible. Values are formed when one confronts and wrestles with truth. Hiding the "seamy" side of life is false protection. Sound instruction based on free choice of reading material is one way to develop character. We seem to be sadly lacking both at home and school in such instruction.

(Mrs.) Mary Lisle King
Mother of Four

"Voice of the People," *Richmond Times-Dispatch,* January 9, 1966, p. 14-B.

Two Books Banned—No Doubt

The only thing not open to debate in Hanover County's book-banning battle today was that "To Kill a Mockingbird" and "1984" no longer were on the bookshelves of county schools.

Hanover's top school officials bluntly blamed the State Board of Education for the county school board action banishing the two modern classics from public school libraries.

The state dodged and weaved and disclaimed responsibility. It said even though the books aren't on its approved list, the decision to ban or not to ban is entirely up to local school boards.

. . .

"If we cannot depend on the competence of the state library committee, who can be depended on for guidance as to what books should be in our schools?" asked Hanover's school board chairman, B. W. Sadler.

"The school board or the superintendent of schools doesn't have the time, nor are we competent, to judge the books," Sadler said. "We are simply trying to set standards for books in the county system."

Policy Change?
"We might change this policy if the state board tells us that their disapproval of any books is not meaningful."

Other books missing from the list, including John Steinbeck's "The Grapes of Wrath" and J. D. Salinger's "The Catcher in the Rye," also will be affected by the school board ruling, Sadler confirmed.

"Voice of the People," *Richmond News-Leader,* January 10, 1966, p. 9.

Who Killed the Mockingbird?

All of today's Forum is given to the beautiful controversy that has blown up since the Hanover County School Board voted unanimously last Tuesday night to ban Harper Lee's Pulitzer Prize–winning novel, *To Kill a Mockingbird.* While the local board's action has a couple of defenders, the overwhelming bulk of the mail reaching us is critical of the decision.

Yet it has become evident that the criticism is missing its mark—or more accurately, is hitting only one of two appropriate targets. The Hanover School Board exhibited the kind of small-bore stupidity that deserves to be roundly condemned; but the Hanover board was merely following the larger stupidity of the State Board of Education.

News stories have made it clear how the incredible system works. Book publishers submit copies of their books to a committee of the State Board of Education. The committee then recommends that some books be approved and some disapproved. Last year 3,361 titles won approval; 1,160 were rejected. Because the State extends grant-in-aid funds to local school boards only for purchase of books on its approved list, the effect is to discourage purchase of books not on the approved list.

Miss Lee's novel, widely acclaimed as a contemporary classic, was submitted for approval in 1960, but rejected. George Orwell's great work,

1984, was approved by the State in 1952, and then removed from the list a year later.

It occurs to us that the fire in this absurd business ought to be shifted from the local board members of Hanover County to the selection committee of the State Board of Education. Who are these dimwitted censors who would deny their sanction to *1984* and *To Kill a Mockingbird*? What credentials, if any, could support such astoundingly bad judgment? Do such board-gauged men as Lewis Powell and Colgate Darden, members of the State Board of Education, condone this nonsense?

Off and on in recent years, we have detected encouraging signs that Virginia was emerging from the peckerwood provincialism and ingrown "morality" that H. L. Mencken, in a famous phrase, attributed to this Sahara of the Bozart. But if this dimwitted committee of the State Board of Education is fairly representative of the wisdom that prevails in high levels of State education policy, Mencken's old indictment stands reconfirmed today. If Messrs. Powell and Darden would like to start the New Year with a signal public service, perhaps they would take the lead in firing this committee and abolishing the State's Index of Approved Books altogether.

Editorial Page, *Richmond News-Leader*, January 10, 1966, p. 10.

Letters and Editor's Comments from "Forum," *Richmond News-Leader*

Editor, *News-Leader*:
Your editorial comments on the action of the Hanover County School Board were very disappointing, to say the least. As a citizen of Hanover and parent of a Lee-Davis student, I am pleased with the action of the Board. Our School Board members and school administrators are interested and concerned with the educational policy for the promotion of the welfare of the children of this county. To establish a reading list of the caliber that would exclude books such as "To Kill a Mockingbird" is an important phase of their welfare. I cannot conceive of this being interpreted as "dim vision," as you termed it.

The book in question is considered as immoral literature and, therefore, is certainly not proper reading for our students. Books on suggested and approved reading lists for high school students should, in my estimation, contribute something or be of some value to a person's education—or why require them to be read? People will always read this type book, but it certainly should never be on a required reading list of a student using his or her time to the best advantage in getting an education for the future. In your defense of the book, you stated it was a best-seller and had been made into a notable movie. This does not give it a stamp of approval. Needless to say, it is read by people everywhere—even Hanover—and more so, now that curiosity has been aroused by publicity. This again does not make it acceptable.

However, this is not the direct cause of my response to your editorial. My reason is to congratulate the Superintendent of Schools, the School Board members, principals and teachers of Hanover County for their efforts and decision in guiding the moral development of our boys and girls. We, as parents, have a tremendous responsibility in the development of our children's moral and spiritual character, as they develop physically. The action taken by our school administrators will have great influence on their moral development. I thank God for them and their vision.

As to your "remedy" of giving 50 copies free to the students of Lee-Davis: I challenge those taking you up on this offer, to write a "Letter to the Editor" and inform us honestly of exactly what the book contributed to their education.

Mrs. L. L. Hollins

Board Acted Wisely in Banning of Novel

Editor, *News-Leader*:

Our radios and TV screens and newspapers of today are constantly overflowing with news of people who are against one thing or the other, but in Wednesday's paper, on the front page was something almost unheard of! Somebody actually had the courage to dare to say that something was immoral.

That in itself made a newsworthy story, and was correctly placed on the front page. On every hand we are told that indecent pictures are not really indecent—they are actually art in its finest form—and if you don't see it that way—then it is because of your nasty little dirty mind. And so most of us are so brainwashed that we say hesitantly, "Well, maybe we are being too harsh," and fall back into a comfortable listlessness.

Such a stand in favor of morality and possibly the reason for our mass spinelessness, is flustrated [sic] by the news that a school board group stood for something smacking of morality, and the paper's editor gives them "what for" on the editorial page. Dare to stand for something and you're publicly ridiculed! And, of course, plain John Q. Citizen doesn't have a widely circulated newspaper with which to withstand such criticism! It's a bit like slapping the face of a man who has his hands tied behind him, isn't it?

The offer to mail the books to students from the Beadle Bumble Fund was so generous that I would like to offer you, absolutely free, a membership in the "Mind Your Own Business Club," established and maintained by a Hanover citizen. Your generosity to us makes me wonder—when the Catholic Church denounces a book or movie, doesn't the Beadle Bumble Fund get frightfully low in cash?

Mrs. Claude E. Tuck

Immoral Actors Side with Students

Editor, *News-Leader*:

How heartening to know that Harper Lee's novel, "To Kill a Mockingbird," has been removed from school library shelves in Hanover County. It's been a nagging worry to realize that our young people were being exposed to a philosophy which says that innocence must be defended; that legal procedures are preferable to mob violence; that in small, southern communities there are heroic people to whom truth and respect for all men are the cornerstones of character. After all, it's a big, cruel world out there, and what youngster has developed sufficient bigotry to withstand the idea that to hurt a less fortunate fellow is as senseless and sad as killing a mockingbird.

We're also reassured to see that our Hanover officials still move without haste when making such a crucial decision, so that the book's offensiveness became obvious only after five years of availability on these same shelves. Do you suppose there's some sort of memory-erasing machine that could remove injurious impressions from those who have already read it?

There may, of course, be some recalcitrant teen-agers who will insist upon taking Miss Lee's book out behind the fence to read. Since theater people have, through the ages, been notoriously immoral, we offer to these few not only our copy, but the fence as well.

The *News-Leader*, too, is certainly subject to censure for making the Beadle Bumble Fund available to Lee-Davis truants who wish to own paperback editions of the book. But let us not add discrimination to immorality. What about the students at Hanover's second high school, Patrick Henry?

Muriel McAuley, David and Nancy Kilgore
Barksdale Theatre, Hanover C. H.

Thanks to generous contributions, the Beadle Bumble Fund has been able to extend its benefactions to Patrick Henry High School also. A number of Patrick Henry students already have written for their free copies; and while the supply lasts, all requests from Hanover high school students will be filled.

Editor

Zealots Shield Students from Good Literature

Editor, *News-Leader*:

Unfortunately, performances such as the Hanover County Board's banning of "To Kill a Mockingbird" are repeated far too often by those overzealous, self-appointed protectors of our morals.

Such was the case a short time ago when the dramatics department of Thomas Jefferson was almost prevented from using the words "sex-starved cobra" in their production of "The Man Who Came to Dinner."

When are these zealots going to realize that the only thing they are "shielding" the students from is good literature?

I am confident that most students are mature enough to read about the shadier side of life without being permanently perverted.

Michael K. Tobias

N.C. State University

"Mockingbird" Not Alone on List of Banned Books

Editor, *News-Leader*:

I enthusiastically applaud and concur with your comments concerning the removal of "To Kill a Mockingbird" from Hanover County school libraries. I have long held that the only Mockingbird which deserves to be killed is the one which screeches outside my window at some ungodly hour every morning, but the board's move came as no great surprise. Nor would it have surprised anyone who generally reads bulletins posted in Virginia public libraries.

These official guardians of literary morality enshrined on the State Library Board (or whatever it is) have, I am sure, produced some ethical gems in the past. Now they have turned again upon children and really outdone themselves. Among the latest batch ordered removed from circulation in public libraries one will find the Tom Swift series, the Hardy Boys' series, the Uncle Wiggly series, the "Wizard of Oz" (shame on Judy Garland), and, no kidding, "The Bobbsey Twins."

We are informed that these books, among others named, constitute cheap sensationalism. God, what a twisted kid I must have been! I actually enjoyed them! And I still can't even rationalize how they contributed significantly to my complete degeneration. My sympathy to Dick and Jane.

Bruce S. Campbell

Virginia Beach

Richmond News-Leader, January 10, 1966, p. 10.

Letters from "Forum," Richmond News-Leader

Suggests Other Books for Possible Banning

Editor, *News-Leader*:

Regarding the removal of "To Kill a Mockingbird" from the library shelves of the Hanover schools, I suggest the Hanover County School Board check closely into "Rebecca of Sunny Brook Farm." Also, I thought that several passages in "Five Little Peppers and How They Grew" were pretty gamey.

Howard Taylor

Immoral Literature Is Sign of Moral Decay

Editor, *News-Leader*:

I am surprised, shocked, and dismayed that you are not supporting the efforts of our police, school boards, and churches to prevent immoral literature from corrupting our young people. Did not Senator Goldwater warn us in 1964 that its spread is another sign of moral decay in our country?

I would suppose your personal influence and that of your paper would be directed against it, and that you would be among the last to adopt the liberal line of "Anything goes in a work of art."

W. H. Buck
Junction City, Kansas

Richmond News-Leader, January 12, 1966, p. 8.

Letters and Comments from *Richmond News-Leader*

Book Ban in Hanover Gets More Attention

Still more reaction has cropped up to the Hanover County school board's banning of two highly praised novels from the county's schools.

In developments reported yesterday:

• The county's executive secretary, Rosewell Page, Jr., a former school board member, attacked the board's action and called on members to rescind it.

• The Ashland Ministers Association resolved to ask the General Assembly to clarify the functions of the state library committee's book list. Further, the ministers called for expressed authority to be given to local school boards to select books not on the approved list. (Legally, local boards may do this. But the Hanover board, in ordering removal of "To Kill a Mockingbird" and "1984," based its action on the fact that the former was rejected by the state and the latter removed from the list.)

•Faculties at Lee-Davis and Patrick Henry high schools, the county's two predominantly white secondary schools, declared that they should have been consulted before such a book selection policy was adopted.

Page said it is impossible to rear a child to choose good and evil "if his experience, gained through the reading of books, is to be hampered in such a manner."

The State Department of Education and the Hanover school board "in their wisdom" might consider banning parts of the Old and New Testaments and numerous literary classics, Page said.

(A spokesman for the State Department of Education, in response to a reporter's query, confirmed that the Bible is on the approved state list.)

Raps School Officials for Banning Book

Chairman B. W. Sadler of the Hanover School Board has finally said something close to the heart of the issue in this book-banning fiasco. "The school board or the superintendent of schools has not the time, nor are we competent to judge the books" (*Times-Dispatch*, January 10).

Since both "1984" and "To Kill a Mockingbird" are short and easy to read, it takes little time to read them—probably less time than it takes to defend having banned them. And it is appalling to realize that the men who banned these books refuse to invest that little time that might give them some idea of what they have done.

More appalling, however, and more relevant to the issue, is that, as Sadler says, the School Board is not competent to judge the books. Yet these are two fairly clear and simple works of fiction. If the board members are incompetent to judge the books, can they be competent to set educational policies for the public schools of an entire county? I think not. Most fiction, including "1984" and "To Kill a Mockingbird," is written for general consumption, not for specialized scholars. Anyone who can read can read it; anyone who can reason can judge it. Sadler's statement implies that the Hanover School Board and school superintendent can neither read nor reason. If this is true, steps should be taken to remedy the situation.

(Mrs.) Christina H. Halsted

Reassured by Board's Decision to Ban Book

The Hanover County School Board has taken a firm stand against "slummy" books. When "new English" is accepted as a part of the curriculum along with "new math," "To Kill a Mockingbird" will hardly find a place in any school library. The main characteristic of "new English" is the use of literature from the first grade through high school. Fictionalized court records and case studies in sociology do not meet the established standards for high school fiction, regardless of the fine craftsmanship they illustrate or the prizes they have won.

Literature is used in school to help students develop the right attitude toward life, as well as to improve reading comprehension, build vocabularies, and to supply new ideas. It is doubtful that a judge in a Virginia court would try a case like the one in "To Kill a Mockingbird" with young people in the audience. And, no parent who cares about the character of his son would send him out with the hero of "Catcher in the Rye" to learn the ways of the world. It is true that many of the novels which have stood the test of time and are regarded as classics depict unfavorable scenes and bad characters. But they are plainly labeled as bad and show the disadvantages of unacceptable social behavior. The current books under discussion fail to do this.

. . .

Our selection committee prevents the stocking of library shelves with books purchased with taxpayers' money to discredit the American way of life and the principles of good taste. . . . If this is censorship, I am for it.

(Mrs.) Noral Miller Turman
Parksley School Librarian

Richmond News-Leader, January 14, 1966, p. 6.

Letter from "Voice of the People," *Richmond Times-Dispatch*

Not All "Classics" Are Fit for Juveniles

As a writer of sixteen published books, including two for children, I heartily support the State Department of Education's policy in withholding state funds from local school authorities for the purchase of books not on the department's approved list. This does not ban the book, since local school boards may acquire any volume they want, provided they use local funds.

The policy, therefore, is not an exercise of censorship, but one of guidance sorely needed in a time when pruriency—occasionally admittedly accompanied by some literary merit—floods the bookstores.

A certain maturity of mind is required for appreciation of genuine literary worth. None at all is needed to produce adolescent snickers or a potentially harmful excitement at the discovery of a phrase or a passage on page so-and-so. Such books, after being awhile in any library, tend to fall open at such well-thumbed pages.

It should be obvious to all Virginians that a measure of restraint or control—call it "guidance" again—must be exercised toward public school library selections. If no line at all were drawn, the titles might conceivably include a new edition of Henry Miller, or "The Memoirs of a Lady of Pleasure" (better known, but not favorably, as "Fanny Hill").

The fact that a book has become a "classic" does not necessarily make it fit for juvenile reading; the fact that it is on the best-seller list, or has been awarded literary prizes, or made into a motion picture, is even less reason to make it so.

It is true that cheap trash is available to the young, in cheap paperbacks, at too many newsstands and corner drugstores. This problem is out of the hands of all the school authorities, state and local. Here the guidance must come from the parents and the homes.

No one man, in a long lifetime, could possibly read all the good, clean, entertaining and constructive books that have been printed in the five centuries since Gutenberg allegedly invented movable type. Let the parents, then, begin at the ABC stage to inculcate a love for such reading in the minds and hearts of their children. Neither the State Department of Education nor the school librarian can do this.

Allan R. Bosworth
Captain, U.S. Navy (ret.), Roanoke

Richmond Times-Dispatch, January 18, 1966, p. 14.

Letters and Editor's Comments from "Forum," *Richmond News-Leader*

Agrees with Decision to Ban Book in Hanover

Editor, *News-Leader*:
As a regular reader of your paper I am very disappointed in your recent position regarding a certain book in a Hanover County school. I have not read the book (nor do I intend to do so) but I did see the diabolical movie, which was repulsive enough. No doubt, had I read the book, I should have found a

rather detailed and descriptive account of what actually took place in the story.

The decision of our School Board does not deny anyone the right to purchase this controversial book, nor any other book, if he so desires.

In our community, Mr. Bosher is a respected businessman of irreproachable character. Were there more such officials of his caliber in the "driver's seat" of the local, state, and federal government of this nation, the rampant moral decline with which we are currently oppressed might have been avoided.

Someone had the audacity to refer to Mr. Bosher as "ignorant." This term is employed today, often indiscriminately by some folks who attempt to categorize those who disagree with them. All of us are ignorant of various matters.

To put so much emphasis on the fact that the author of "To Kill a Mockingbird" was awarded the Pulitzer Prize does not impress me. Martin Luther King was awarded the Nobel Peace Prize. What irony!

I am thankful that at an early age my parents introduced me to wholesome reading material. Consequently, never having cultivated an appetite for the baser literature (and I use the word "literature" loosely), I have always sought undefiled reading matter.

I don't recall that such a commotion as this came about when an atheist in Maryland carried to the federal courts her protest against the use of prayer in the public schools.

Everyone should be cognizant of the fact that a young mind is a flexible and a vulnerable mind. Therefore, influences such as books, movies, etc. can either elevate or degrade that mind.

It takes a strong back to stand up and be counted. May I say, bravo, Mr. Bosher! Carry on!

Miss Vivian Blake

Author Harper Lee Comments on Book-Banning

Editor, *News-Leader*:

Recently I have received echoes down this way of the Hanover County School Board's activities, and what I've heard makes me wonder if any of its members can read.

Surely it is plain to the simplest intelligence that "To Kill a Mockingbird" spells out in words of seldom more than two syllables a code of honor and conduct, Christian in its ethic, that is the heritage of all Southerners. To hear that the novel is "immoral" has made me count the years between now and 1984, for I have yet to come across a better example of doublethink.

I feel, however, that the problem is one of illiteracy, not Marxism. Therefore I enclose a small contribution to the Beadle Bumble Fund that I hope will be used to enroll the Hanover County School Board in any first grade of its choice.

Harper Lee
Monroeville, Ala.

*In most controversies, the lady is expected to have the last word. In this particular discussion, it seems especially fitting that the last word should come from the lady who wrote "To Kill a Mockingbird." With Miss Lee's letter, we call a halt, at least temporarily, to the publication of letters commenting on the book-banning in Hanover County.

Editor

Richmond News-Leader, January 15, 1966, p. 10.

FRED ERISMAN

The Romantic Regionalism of Harper Lee

When Mark Twain stranded the steamboat *Walter Scott* on a rocky point in Chapter 13 of *Huckleberry Finn*, he rounded out an attack on Southern romanticism begun in *Life on the Mississippi*. There, as every reader knows, he asserted that Sir Walter Scott's novels of knighthood and chivalry had done "measureless harm" by infecting the American South with "the jejune romanticism of an absurd past that is dead." This premise does not stop with Twain. W. J. Cash, writing almost sixty years later, continues the assertion, observing that the South, already nostalgic in the early nineteenth century, "found perhaps the most perfect expression for this part of its spirit in the cardboard medievalism of the Scotch novels." As recently as 1961, W. R. Taylor, in *Cavalier and Yankee*, several times alludes to Scott as he traces the development of the myth of the planter aristocracy.

For these three men, and for many like them, Southern romanticism has been a pernicious, backward-looking belief. It has, they imply, mired the South in a stagnant morass of outdated ideas, from which there is little chance of escape. A more hopeful view, however, appears in Harper Lee's novel of Alabama life, *To Kill a Mockingbird* (1960). Miss Lee is well aware of traditional Southern romanticism and, indeed, agrees that it was and is a pervasive influence in the South; one of the subtlest allusions in the entire novel comes in Chapter 11, as the Finch children read *Ivanhoe* to the dying

From *The Alabama Review* XXVI:2 (April 1973). © 1973 by The University of Alabama Press.

but indomitable Southern lady, Mrs. Henry Lafayette Dubose. At the same time, she sees in the New South—the South of 1930–1935—the dawning of a newer and more vital form of romanticism. She does not see this newer romanticism as widespread, nor does she venture any sweeping predictions as to its future. Nevertheless, in *To Kill a Mockingbird*, Miss Lee presents an Emersonian view of Southern romanticism, suggesting that the South can move from the archaic, imported romanticism of its past toward the more reasonable, pragmatic, and native romanticism of a Ralph Waldo Emerson. If the movement can come to maturity, she implies, the South will have made a major step toward becoming truly regional in its vision.

As Miss Lee unfolds her account of three years in the lives of Atticus, Jem, and Scout Finch, and in the history of Maycomb, Alabama, she makes clear the persistence of the old beliefs. Maycomb, she says, is "an old town, . . . a tired old town," even "an ancient town." A part of southern Alabama from the time of the first settlements, and isolated and largely untouched by the Civil War, it was, like the South, turned inward upon itself by Reconstruction. Indeed, its history parallels that of the South in so many ways that it emerges as a microcosm of the South. This quality is graphically suggested by the Maycomb County courthouse, which dominates the town square:

> The Maycomb County courthouse was faintly reminiscent of Arlington in one respect: the concrete pillars supporting its south roof were too heavy for their light burden. The pillars were all that remained standing when the original courthouse burned in 1856. Another courthouse was built around them. It is better to say, built in spite of them. But for the south porch, the Maycomb County courthouse was early Victorian, presenting an unoffensive vista when seen from the north. From the other side, however, Greek revival columns clashed with a big nineteenth-century clock tower housing a rusty unreliable instrument, a view indicating a people determined to preserve every physical scrap of the past.

Miss Lee's courthouse, inoffensive from the north but architecturally appalling from the south, neatly summarizes Maycomb's reluctance to shed the past. It is, like the South, still largely subject to the traditions of the past.

The microcosmic quality of Maycomb suggested by its courthouse appears in other ways, as well. The town's social structure, for example, is characteristically Southern. Beneath its deceptively placid exterior, Maycomb has a taut, well-developed caste system designed to separate whites from blacks. If Maycomb's caste system is not so openly oppressive as that of

John Dollard's "Southerntown" (where "caste has replaced slavery as a means of maintaining the essence of the old status order in the South"), it still serves the same end—to keep the blacks in their place. The operations of this system are obvious. First Purchase African M. E. Church, for example, "the only church in Maycomb with a steeple and bell," is subjected to minor but consistent desecration: "Negroes worshiped in it on Sundays and white men gambled in it on weekdays." The whites, moreover, clearly expect deferential behavior of the blacks. One of the good ladies of the Methodist missionary circle interrupts her paeans to Christian fellowship to remark, "There's nothing more distracting than a sulky darky. . . . Just ruins your day to have one of 'em in the kitchen." The Finch children, attending church with Calpurnia, their black housekeeper, are confronted with doffed hats and "weekday gestures of respectful attention." And, in the most telling commentary of all upon the pervasive pressures of the caste system, when Calpurnia accompanies Atticus Finch to convey the news of Tom Robinson's death, she must ride in the back seat of the automobile.

Even more indicative of Maycomb's characteristically Southern caste system is the power of the sexual taboo, which has been called "the strongest taboo of the system." This is dramatized by the maneuverings during Tom Robinson's trial of allegedly raping Mayella Ewell, a central episode in the novel. Although Tom's infraction of the black man-white woman code is demonstrated to have been false, he is nonetheless condemned. The caste taboo outweighs empirical evidence. As Atticus says later of the jury, "Those are twelve reasonable men in everyday life, Tom's jury, but you saw something come between them and reason. . . . There's something in our world that makes men lose their heads—they couldn't be fair if they tried." Despite the presence of a more than reasonable doubt as to his guilt, despite the discrediting of the Ewells, the chief witnesses for the prosecution, Tom Robinson is condemned. As Atticus points out, the entire prosecution is based upon "the assumption—the evil assumption—that *all* Negroes lie, that *all* Negroes are basically immoral beings, that *all* Negro men are not to be trusted around our women." Tom's conviction is mute testimony to the strength of that caste-oriented assumption.

Another illustration of Maycomb's archetypal Southernness that is as typical as its caste system is the ubiquitous system of class distinctions among the whites. Miss Lee's characters fall readily into four classes, ranging from the "old aristocracy" represented by Atticus Finch's class-conscious sister, Alexandra, to the poor white trash represented by Bob Ewell and his brood, who have been "the disgrace of Maycomb for three generations." In presenting the interaction of these classes, she gives a textbook demonstration of the traditional social stratification of the American South.

The upper-class-consciousness so manifest in Aunt Alexandra appears most strongly in her regard for "family," a concern that permeates Part II of *To Kill a Mockingbird*. Like the small-town aristocrats described in Allison Davis's *Deep South*, she has a keen appreciation of the "laterally extended kin group." Although the complex interrelationships of Maycomb society are generally known to the Finch children, it is Aunt Alexandra who drives home their social significance. After a series of social gaffes by Scout, Aunt Alexandra prevails upon Atticus to lecture the children concerning their status. This he does, in his most inflectionless manner:

> 'Your aunt has asked me to try and impress upon you and Jean Louise that you are not from run-of-the-mill people, that you are the product of several generations' gentle breeding . . . and that you should try to live up to your name. . . . She asked me to tell you you must try to behave like the little lady and gentleman that you are. She wants to talk to you about the family and what it's meant to Maycomb County through the years, so you'll have some idea of who you are, so you might be moved to behave accordingly.'

In her insistence that family status be preserved, Aunt Alexandra typifies the family-oriented aristocrat of the Old South.

No less well developed is Miss Lee's emphasis upon the subtleties of class distinction. In this, too, she defines Maycomb as a characteristically Southern community. It has its upper class, in Aunt Alexandra, in the members of the Missionary Society, and in the town's professional men—Atticus, Dr. Reynolds, Judge Taylor, and so on. It has its middle class, in the numerous faceless and often nameless individuals who flesh out Miss Lee's story— Braxton Underwood, the owner-editor of *The Maycomb Tribune*, or Mr. Sam Levy, who shamed the Ku Klux Klan in 1920 by proclaiming that "he'd sold 'em the very sheets on their backs." It has its lower class, generically condemned by Aunt Alexandra as "trash," but sympathetically presented in characters like Walter Cunningham, one of the Cunninghams of Old Sarum, a breed of men who "hadn't taken anything from or off of anybody since they migrated to the New World." Finally, it has its dregs, the Ewells, who, though more slovenly than the supposedly slovenliest of the blacks, still possess the redeeming grace of a white skin. These distinctions Aunt Alexandra reveres and protects, as when she remarks, "You can scrub Walter Cunningham till he shines, you can put him in shoes and a new suit, but he'll never be like Jem. . . . Because—he—is—trash." For Aunt Alexandra, the class gap between the Finches and the Cunninghams is one that can never be bridged.

The existence of a caste system separating black from white, or of a well-developed regard for kin-group relations, or of a system of class stratification is, of course, not unique. But, from the simultaneous existence of these three systems, and from the way in which they dominate Maycomb attitudes, emerges the significance of Maycomb's antiquity. It is a representation of the Old South, still clinging, as in its courthouse, to every scrap of the past. Left alone, it would remain static, moldering away as surely as John Brown's body. So too, Miss Lee suggests, may the South. This decay, however, can be prevented. In her picture of the New South and the New Southerner, Miss Lee suggests how a decadently romantic tradition can be transformed into a functional romanticism and how, from this change, can come a revitalizing of the South.

The "New South" that Harper Lee advocates is new only by courtesy. In one respect—the degree to which it draws upon the romantic idealism of an Emerson—it is almost as old as the Scottish novels so lacerated by Mark Twain; in another, it is even older, as it at times harks back to the Puritan ideals of the seventeenth century. By the standards of the American South of the first third of the twentieth century, however, it is new, for it flies in the face of much that traditionally characterizes the South. With Emerson, it spurns the past, looking instead to the reality of the present. With him, it places principled action above self-interest, willingly accepting the difficult consequences of a right decision. It recognizes, like both Emerson and the Puritans, the diversity of mankind, yet recognizes also that this diversity is unified by a set of "higher laws" that cannot be ignored. In short, in the several Maycomb townspeople who see through the fog of the past, and who act not from tradition but from principle, Miss Lee presents the possible salvation of the South.

Foremost among these people is Atticus Finch, attorney for the central character of Miss Lee's novel. Though himself a native of Maycomb, a member of one of the oldest families in the area, and "related by blood or marriage to nearly every family in the town," Atticus is not the archetypal Southerner that his sister has become. Instead, he is presented as a Southern version of Emersonian man, the individual who vibrates to his own iron string, the one man in the town that the community trusts "to do right," even as they deplore his peculiarities. Through him, and through Jem and Scout, the children he is rearing according to his lights, Miss Lee presents her view of the New South.

That Atticus Finch is meant to be an atypical Southerner is plain; Miss Lee establishes this from the beginning, as she reports that Atticus and his brother are the first Finches to leave the family lands and study elsewhere. This atypical quality, however, is developed even further. Like Emerson,

Atticus recognizes that his culture is retrospective, groping "among the dry bones of the past . . . [and putting] the living generation into masquerade out of its faded wardrobe." He had no hostility toward his past; he is not one of the alienated souls so beloved of Southern Gothicists. He does, though, approach his past and its traditions with a tolerant skepticism. His attitude toward "old family" and "gentle breeding" has already been suggested. A similar skepticism is implied by his repeated observation that "you never really understand a person until you consider things from his point of view . . . until you climb into his skin and walk around in it." He understands the difficulties of Tom Robinson, although Tom Robinson is black; he understands the difficulties of a Walter Cunningham, though Cunningham is—to Aunt Alexandra—"trash"; he understands the pressures being brought to bear upon his children because of his own considered actions. In each instance he acts according to his estimate of the merits of the situation, striving to see that each receives justice. He is, in short, as Edwin Bruell has suggested, "no heroic type but any graceful, restrained, simple person like one from Attica." Unfettered by the corpse of the past, he is free to live and work as an individual.

This freedom to act he does not gain easily. Indeed, he, like Emerson's nonconformist, frequently finds himself whipped by the world's displeasure. And yet, like Emerson's ideal man, when faced by this harassment and displeasure, he has "the habit of magnanimity and religion to treat it godlike as a trifle of no concernment." In the development of this habit he is aided by a strong regard for personal principle, even as he recognizes the difficulty that it brings to his life and the lives of his children. This is established early in the novel, with the introduction of the Tom Robinson trial. When the case is brought up by Scout, following a fight at school, Atticus responds, "'If I didn't [defend Tom Robinson] I couldn't hold up my head in town, I couldn't represent this county in the legislature, I couldn't even tell you or Jem not to do something again. . . . Scout, simply by the nature of the work, every lawyer gets at least one case in his lifetime that affects him personally. This one's mine, I guess.'" He returns to this theme later, observing that "'This case . . . is something that goes to the essence of a man's conscience—Scout, I couldn't go to church and worship God if I didn't try to help that man.'" Scout points out that opinion among the townspeople runs counter to this, whereupon Atticus replies, "'They're certainly entitled to think that, and they're entitled to full respect for their opinions . . . but before I can live with other folks I've got to live with myself. The one thing that doesn't abide by majority rule is a person's conscience." No careful ear is needed to hear the echoes of Emerson's "Nothing can bring you peace but yourself. Nothing can bring you peace but the triumph of principles." In his heeding both principle and conscience, whatever the cost to himself, Atticus is singularly Emersonian.

The Emersonian quality of Atticus's individualism is emphasized in two additional ways—through his awareness of the clarity of the childhood vision (suggesting Emerson's remark that "the sun illuminates only the eye of the man, but shines into the eye and the heart of the child. The lover of nature is he . . . who has retained the spirit of infancy even into the era of manhood."), and through his belief in the higher laws of life. The first of these appears at least three times throughout the novel. Early in the Tom Robinson sequence, an attempted lynching is thwarted by the sudden appearance of the Finch children, leading Atticus to observe, "'So it took an eight-year-old child to bring 'em to their senses, didn't it? . . . Hmp, maybe we need a police force of children . . . you children last night made Walter Cunningham stand in my shoes for a minute. That was enough.'" The view is reinforced by the comments of Dolphus Raymond, the town drunk, who sees in the children's reaction to the trial the unsullied operations of instinct. And, thus suggested, it is made explicitly by Atticus himself, as, following Tom Robinson's conviction, he tells Jem: "'If you had been on that jury, son, and eleven other boys like you, Tom would be a free man. . . . So far nothing in your life has interfered with your reasoning process.'" The point could not be more obvious; in the unsophisticated vision of the child is a perception of truth that most older, tradition-bound people have lost. Atticus, like Emerson's lover of nature, has retained it, and can understand it; it only remains for that vision to be instilled in others.

Linked to this belief is Atticus's recognition of the diversity of man and his faith in the higher laws—although, significantly, his higher laws are not the abstruse, cosmic laws of Emerson, but the practical laws of the courts. Atticus, by his own confession, is no idealist, believing in the absolute goodness of mankind. In his courtroom argument he acknowledges his belief that "'there is not a person . . . who has never told a lie, who has never done an immoral thing, and there is no man living who has never looked upon a woman without desire.'" To this he adds his recognition of the randomness of life: "'Some people are smarter than others, some people have more opportunity because they're born with it, some men make more money than others, some ladies make better cakes than others—some people are born gifted beyond the normal scope of most men.'" At the same time, he also believes that these flawed, diverse people are united by one thing—the law. There is, he says, "'one way in this country in which all men are created equal—there is one human institution that makes a pauper the equal of a Rockefeller, the stupid man the equal of an Einstein, and the ignorant man

the equal of any college president. That institution, gentlemen, is a court.'"
In this, his climactic speech to the jury, Atticus makes clear his commitment.
Like the Puritans, he assumes the flawed nature of man, but, like Emerson,
he looks to the higher laws—those of the court and of the nation—that
enable man to transcend his base diversity and give him the only form of
equality possible in a diverse society. Like the Emerson of the "Ode to Chan-
ning," he argues:

> Let man serve law for man;
> Live for friendship, live for love;
> For truth's and harmony's behoof;
> The state may follow how it can.

Atticus will, indeed, serve law for man, leaving the state—his contempo-
raries—to follow how it can. He, at least, has absolved him to himself.

Throughout *To Kill a Mockingbird*, Harper Lee presents a dual view of
the American South. On the one hand, she sees the South as still in the grip
of the traditions and habits so amply documented by Davis, Dollard, and
others—caste division along strictly color lines, hierarchical class stratification within castes, and exaggerated regard for kin-group relations within
particular classes, especially the upper and middle classes of the white caste.
On the other hand, she argues that the South has within itself the potential
for progressive change, stimulated by the incorporation of the New England
romanticism of an Emerson, and characterized by the pragmatism, principles, and wisdom of Atticus Finch. If, as she suggests, the South can exchange
its old romanticism for the new, it can modify its life to bring justice and
humanity to all of its inhabitants, black and white alike.

In suggesting the possibility of a shift from the old romanticism to the
new, however, Miss Lee goes even further. If her argument is carried to its
logical extension, it becomes apparent that she is suggesting that the South,
by assimilating native (though extra-regional) ideals, can transcend the
confining sectionalism that has dominated it in the past, and develop the
breadth of vision characteristic of the truly regional outlook. This outlook,
which Lewis Mumford calls a "soundly bottomed regionalism," is one that
"can achieve cosmopolitan breadth without fear of losing its integrity or
virtue: it is only a sick and puling regionalism that must continually gaze with
enamored eyes upon its own face, praising its warts and pimples as beauty
marks. For a genuine regional tradition lives by two principles. One is, *culti-
vate whatever you have*, no matter how poor it is; it is at least your own. The
other is, *seek elsewhere for what you do not possess*; absorb whatever is good
wherever you may find it; *make it your own*." If the South can relinquish its

narcissistic regard for the warts and pimples of its past, it can take its place among the regions of the nation and the world.

Miss Lee sees such a development as a distinct possibility. Maycomb, in the past isolated and insulated, untouched by even the Civil War, is no longer detached from the outside world. It is, as Miss Lee suggests through the Finch brothers' going elsewhere to study, beginning to seek for what it does not possess. (This quest, however, is no panacea, as Miss Lee implies with the character of the pathetically inept Miss Caroline Fisher, the first-grade teacher from North Alabama, who introduces the "Dewey Decimal System" to revolutionize the Maycomb County School System.) Moreover, Maycomb is being forced to respond to events touching the nation and the world. The Depression is a real thing, affecting the lives of white and black alike; the merchants of Maycomb are touched by the fall of the National Recovery Act; and Hitler's rise to power and his persecution of the Jews make the power of Nazism apparent even to the comfortable Christians of the town. Maycomb, in short, like the South it represents, is becoming at last a part of the United States; what affects the nation affects it, and the influence of external events can no longer be ignored.

The organic links of Maycomb with the world at large extend even further, as Miss Lee goes on to point out the relationship between what happens in Maycomb and the entirety of human experience. The novel opens and closes on a significant note—that life in Maycomb, despite its Southern particularity, is an integral part of human history. This broadly regional vision appears in the first paragraphs of the novel, as the narrator, the mature Scout, reflects upon the events leading up to the death of Bob Ewell:

> I maintain that the Ewells started it all, but Jem, who was four years my senior, said it started long before that. He said it began the summer Dill came to us, when Dill first gave us the idea of making Boo Radley come out.
>
> I said if he wanted to take a broad view of the thing, it really began with Andrew Jackson. If General Jackson hadn't run the Creeks up the creek, Simon Finch would never have paddled up the Alabama, and where would we be if he hadn't? We were far too old to settle an argument with a fist-fight, so we consulted Atticus. Our father said we were both right.

The theme of this passage—that events of long ago and far away can have consequences in the present—is echoed at the novel's end. Tom Robinson is dead, Bob Ewell is dead, Boo Radley has emerged and submerged, and

Scout, aged nine, is returning home. The view from the Radley porch evokes a flood of memories, which, for the first time, fall into a coherent pattern for her: the complex interaction of three years of children's play and adult tragedy is revealed in a single, spontaneous moment of intuitive perception. "Just standing on the Radley porch was enough," she says. "As I made my way home, I felt very old. . . . As I made my way home, I thought what a thing to tell Jem tomorrow. . . . As I made my way home I thought Jem and I would get grown but there wasn't much else left for us to learn, except possibly algebra." She has learned, with Emerson, that "to the young mind everything is individual. . . . By and by, it finds how to join two things and see in them one nature; then three, then three thousand; and so, tyrannized over by its own unifying instinct, it goes on tying things together . . . [discovering] that these objects are not chaotic, and are not foreign, but have a law which is also a law of the human mind." When the oneness of the world dawns upon a person, truly all that remains is algebra.

Miss Lee's convictions could not be more explicit. The South, embodied here in Maycomb and its residents, can no longer stand alone and apart. It must recognize and accept its place in national and international life, and it must accept the consequences for doing so. It must recognize and accept that adjustments must come, that other ways of looking at things are perhaps better than the traditional ones. Like Emerson's individual, it must be no longer hindered by the name of goodness, but must explore if it be goodness. If, to a perceptive and thoughtful observer, the old ways have lost their value, new ones must be found to supplant them; if, on the other hand, the old ways stand up to the skeptical eye, they should by all means be preserved. This Atticus Finch has done, and this he is teaching his children to do. By extension, the South must do the same, cultivating the good that it possesses, but looking elsewhere for the good that it lacks. Only in this way can it escape the stifling provincialism that has characterized its past, and take its place as a functioning region among human regions. If the South can learn this fundamental lesson, seeking its unique place in relation to human experience, national experience, and world experience, all that will remain for it, too, will be algebra.

R.A. DAVE

To Kill a Mockingbird: *Harper Lee's Tragic Vision*

To Kill a Mockingbird is quite an ambiguous title, the infinitive leaving a wide scope for a number of adverbial queries—how, when, where, and, of course, *why*—all leading to intriguing speculation and suspense. One is left guessing whether it is a crime-thriller or a book on bird-hunting. Look at it any way, the title hurts the reader's sensibility and creates an impression that something beautiful is being bruised and broken. It is only after he plunges into the narrative and is swept off into its current that he starts gathering the significance of the title. After buying the gift of an air gun for his little son, Atticus says: 'I would rather you shot at tin cans in the backyard, but I know you will go after birds . . . but remember, it's a sin to kill a mockingbird.' And when Scout asks Miss Maudie about it, for that is the only time when she ever heard her father say it is a sin to do something, she replies saying:

> 'Your father is right. Mockingbirds don't do one thing but make music for us to enjoy. They don't eat up people's gardens, don't nest in corncribs, they don't do one thing but sing their hearts out for us. That's why it is a sin to kill a mockingbird.'

And as the words 'it's a sin to kill a mockingbird' keep on echoing into our ears, we are apt to see on their wings the mockingbirds that will sing all

From *Indian Studies in American Fiction*. © 1974 by The Macmillan Company of India Limited.

day and even at night without seeming to take time to hunt for worms or insects. At once the moral undertones of the story acquire symbolical expression and the myth of the mockingbird is seen right at the thematic centre of the story. The streets of Maycomb were deserted, the doors and windows were instantaneously shut the moment Calpurnia sent round the word about the dog, gone mad in February not in August. . . . There was hush all over. 'Nothing is more deadly than a deserted waiting street. The trees were silent, the mockingbirds were silent.' During moments of peril, such as these, even the mockingbirds do not sing! That the little girl should see in the dog's march to death some motivation of "an invisible force' is as significant as her being struck by the silence of the mockingbirds. We have several such moments of eloquent silence in the novel. But what is more disturbing is the behaviour of the neighbours, who open their 'windows one by one' only after the danger was over. Atticus could protect them against a mad dog: he could not protect the innocent victim against their madness! As the Finch children along with their friend Dill waver at the portals of the Radley House on their way to solve the Boo mystery, we again hear the solitary singer:

> High above us in the darkness a solitary mocker poured out his repertoire in blissful unawareness of whose tree he sat in, plunging from the shrill kee, kee of the sunflower bird to the irascible qua-ack of a bluejay, to the sad lament of Poor Will, Poor Will, Poor Will.

And when they shoot Tom Robinson, while lost in his unavailing effort to scale the wall in quest of freedom, Mr Underwood, the editor of *The Montgomery Advertiser*, 'likened Tom's death to the senseless slaughter of songbirds by hunters and children.' As we find the mockingbird fluttering and singing time and again, the whole of Maycomb seems to be turning before our eyes into a wilderness full of senseless slaughter. The mockingbird motif, as effective as it is ubiquitous, and a continual reminder of the thematic crux, comes alive in the novel with all its associations of innocence, joy, and beauty.

The mockingbird myth is there in American literature and folklore. In Walt Whitman's "Out of the Cradle Endlessly Rocking", we have a tender tale of mockingbirds, the tale of love and longing and loss. . . . The mockingbird myth is most powerfully used by Whitman, who travels back and forth on the waves of childhood memories with a mist of tears through which 'a man, yet by these tears a little boy again', sings a reminiscence. The mockingbird symbol in the novel acquires a profound moral significance. For, unlike the world of tender love and longing of Walt Whitman's Alabama birds, Harper Lee's Alabama presents a bleak picture of a narrow world torn by hatred, injustice, violence and cruelty, and we lament to see 'what man has made of man'. It brings out forcefully the condition of Negro subculture in the white world where a Negro, as dark as a mockingbird, is accepted largely as a servant or at best as an entertainer. But apart from the symbolical identity, *To Kill a Mockingbird* has an astonishing technical kinship with Whitman's "Out of the Cradle Endlessly Rocking". Both, Whitman and Harper Lee, recollect childhood memories after many years have gone by. In both, the poem and the novel, we see a parabolic pattern. After years, the narrator goes back into the past, swimming across a flood of memories, and then comes back floating onwards towards the present moment and beyond. The way childhood memories impinge on adult consciousness, turning 'a man, yet by these tears a little boy again', gives a new dimension to the autobiographical mode, and heightens dramatically the reported impressions by the fact that what happens to the artist's consciousness is more important than the actual happening itself. In the novel, Harper Lee instals herself avowedly as the narrator and depicts not only the external world of action, but the internal world of character also.

Harper Lee has a remarkable gift of story-telling. Her art is visual, and with cinematographic fluidity and subtlety we see a scene melting into another scene without jolts of transition. Like Browning's poet, Harper Lee is a 'maker-see'. She unfolds the wide panorama of Maycomb life in such a way that we, the readers, too, get transported in that world within world and watch helplessly, though not quite hopelessly, the bleak shadows of the adult world darkening the children's dream world.

To Kill a Mockingbird is autobiographical not merely in its mode of expression but also in quite a personal sense. If David Copperfield is Charles Dickens and Stephen Dedalus in *A Portrait of the Artist as a Young Man* is James Joyce, Jean Louise Finch (Scout) is unmistakably Harper Lee. If we examine the internal evidence, we can easily infer that in 1935, while Hitler was persecuting the Jews in Germany and Tom Robinson was being tried in Maycomb, Jean Finch Scout, the narrator, was 'not yet nine', perhaps she was born, like her creator, in 1926. The identification between the narrator and the novelist is apparent. The novel with its autobiographical mode strikes a psychological balance between the past, the present, and the future. The writer projects herself into the story as Scout in the present. What she narrates is the past. And as the past is being unfolded the reader wonders how the writer's retrospect will lead her on to the future, which is a continual mystery. This evokes in the novel considerable suspense. We follow the trial of Tom Robinson and the ostracising of the Finch family, holding our breath. But unlike David Copperfield who casts a backward

glance over a long-travelled road or Stephen Dedalus who grows from childhood to youth and to manhood seeking aesthetic vision and development in
exile, Scout Finch concentrates on a single phase, as a moment of crisis in
which childhood innocence was shattered by the terrifying experiences of the
adult world.

It is a memory tale told by a little girl, Jean Louise Finch, called Scout
in the novel. She becomes a mirror of experience and we see reflected in her
the Maycomb world. Her memories recollected in imaginative tranquillity
become a dramatised action and the fiction gets an extraordinary gloss of
veracity. A white girl's accusation of her rape by a Negro causes a huge
upheaval that rocks 'the very old and tired town of Maycomb'. It all began
the summer when Scout was six and her brother Jem ten. We find the Finch
family caught in the storm of the white, popular reaction, but braving it all
with remarkable steadfastness, courage and fortitude. The two motherless
children and their father face the ordeal so heroically that it lifts the story
from the probable melodramatic and sentimental doldrums and makes *To Kill
a Mockingbird*, which is a winter's tale, a heroic one told in a lyric way. Apart
from the mockingbird symbol which is pervasive, we have several other
symbols. When it snows in Maycomb, after years and years, the county
school declares a holiday, and we see the Finch children trying to make a
snow-man. But there is more mud than snow:

> 'Jem, I ain't ever heard of a nigger snowman,' I said.
> 'He won't be black long,' he grunted.

And he tries to cover it with some snow-flakes, making it white. But at
night Miss Maudie's house is on fire, and Scout watches 'our absolute
Morphodite go black and crumble'. The snow-man turning alternately white
and black suggests how frail and skin-deep is the colour. Besides, Miss
Maudie's flowers, too, caught in the flames, symbolise innocence in the grip
of fire. And as we see the yellow flames leaping up in a snowy, dark night we
have the symbols of the white snow and the coloured flames standing for cold
hatred and fiery wrath that might lead to the crack of the world as visualised
by Robert Frost in his poem "Fire and Ice." Symbolism lends poetic touch to
the novel that depicts not only the external world of action but also the
internal world of character. For, here the novelist registers the impact of the
central action not so much on the protagonist as on the others. Both Boo
Radley locked in his own home for fifteen long years for some trifling adolescent pranks so that his father could find the vanity fair of the society conge-
nial, and Tom Robinson sentenced to death for a rape he never committed,
are kept as invisible as the crimes they never committed. Two such innocent

victimisations paralleled with each other intensify the tragic view of the world and recall the terrifying prognosis: 'So shall the world go on: to good men malignant, to bad men benign.' What happens to the innocent victims, who are largely shut out from us like beasts in a cage, is really not as important as the way it stirs the world around. The novel that opens with the theme of persecution taking us back to the ancestor, Simon Finch, who sailed across the Atlantic to escape religious persecution in England, keeps the victims generally off the stage, invisible while the prolonged tensions between the protagonist minority and the antagonist majority shake the small world of Maycomb with an ever increasing emotional and moral disturbance. In this oblique handling of the central theme we have, what Virginia Woolf describes as 'a luminous halo, a semi-transparent envelope'. It is an effective artistic device. All this is presented through the fascinating, though disturbing, flash-backs, and the continual backthrust intensifies the unforgettableness of the narrator's experience.

Maycomb is a microcosm, and the novelist's creative fecundity has peopled it well. We have a cross-section of humanity: men and women, young and old, good and bad, white and black. *To Kill a Mockingbird* presents a memorable portrait gallery. Generally it is the evil characters that are better portrayed than the good, Satan rather than God. But Harper Lee's emotional and moral bias seems to put her more at ease with good people than bad. The wicked characters tend to be hazy whereas the good characters stand out prominently throbbing with life. Bob Ewell and his allies are just paper-figures. Again, the women in the novel are better delineated than the men with the probable exception of Atticus. But her highest achievement in characterisation is manifest in children who at once spring to life. If the successful delineation of children characters is a mark of creative genius, Harper Lee has attained a notable success. Unlike her grown-up characters who easily tend to be caricatures seen in concave and convex mirrors, these children are wonderfully true to life. We have some most unforgettable vignettes. . . . [Think] of Dill getting sick of the trial and breaking down. It is Mr Raymond, the man 'who perpetrated fraud against himself by drinking Coca Cola in a whiskey bag' who says:

'Let him get a little older and he won't get sick and cry. Maybe things will strike him as being—not quite right, say, but he won't cry, not when he gets a few years on him.'

And we have the sad juxtaposition of the two worlds. We have children—Jem, Scout, Dill and the whole lot of them with an insatiable sense of wonder and curiosity. It is they who are bewildered by the ways of the grown-up world and confronted with the most disturbing problems like 'What exactly is a Nigger-lover Atticus?' 'What is rape, Cal?' When Tom Robinson is adjudged to be guilty, it is their young hearts that we see bleeding:

> I shut my eyes. Judge Taylor was polling the jury: 'Guilty . . .
> guilty . . . guilty . . . guilty . . . I pecked at Jem: his hands were
> white from gripping the balcony rail, and his shoulders jerked as
> if each 'guilty' was a separate stab between them.

And here is Atticus, the defence counsel, the hero of the trial scene, but for whom the trial would have seemed as if out of Kafka's world. At least the phantasmal jury and the accusers all seem to have been people who should not have surprised even Joseph K. The trial was over, but not so the heartquakes of the young, although they knew, as Scout points out, 'in the secret courts of men's hearts Atticus had no case'.

> 'Atticus—' said Jem bleakly.
> He turned the door way. 'What, son?'
> 'How could they do it, how could they?'
> 'I don't know, but they did it. They've done it before and they did
> it tonight and they'll do it again, and when they do, it seems that
> only children will weep. Goodnight.'

Atticus is the protagonist, reticent, dignified and distant. When the entire white world seems to have lost its head, it is he who remains sane and firm. He is a wonderful combination of strength and tenderness. He is a stoic and can withstand the ostracism and persecution with almost superhuman courage and fortitude. He is a widower but treats his motherless children with so much affection and understanding that they call him 'Atticus'. They are about his only friends in a world in which he is lonely. It is in the trial scene that we see Atticus at his best, exposing the falsehood and meanness of the white world intent on destroying an innocent Negro. If Jean Scout, the daughter, keeps the wheel of the story turning, Atticus is the axle. He is a man who seems to have been made to approximate to Newman's idea of a gentleman. He never inflicts pain on others, but strives to relieve them of it even at the cost of his own and his children's suffering. It is a highly idealised character. He stands up like a lighthouse, firm, noble, and magnanimous.

But the children and Atticus, with a few other probable exceptions like Calpurnia and Sheriff Tate, and the victims are about the only normal fold in the novel. These Maycomb women are quite funny. They are the comic characters in a tragic world; they play the chorus in the novel. Here is Aunt Alexandra, 'analogous to Mount Everest . . . she was cold and there', betraying the novelist's eye for the ridiculous:

> She was not fat, but solid, and she chose protective garments that drew up her bosom to giddy heights, inched in her waist, flared out her rear, and managed to suggest that Aunt Alexandra's was once an hour-glass figure. From any angle it was formidable.

We have 'Miss Stephanie Crawford, that English channel of gossip', and Miss Dubose who was horrible: 'Her face was horrible. Her face was the color of a dirty pillow-case, and the corners of her mouth glistened.' But Calpurnia, the nurse, who reminds us of Dilsey in Faulkner's *The Sound and the Fury*, and Miss Maudie are the only two women who have beneath their tough exteriors abundant humanity. Calpurnia, who leads a double-life, takes Jem and Scout to the Negro church the way Dilsey takes Benjy to the Easter service in Faulkner. Here we are in the church; the novelist has almost actually taken us in:

> The warm bitter sweet smell of clean Negro welcomed us as we entered the churchyard—Hearts of Love hair-dressing mingled with asafoetida, snuff, Hoyt's Cologne, Brown's Mule, peppermint, and lilac talcum.

But there is a counterpoint. Lula, a Negro, protests against the visit of the white children; and Calpurnia retorts: 'It's the same God, ain't it?' Calpurnia has brought up these motherless children. It is the persons like Atticus and Calpurnia who try to bridge the chasm dividing the whites from the blacks. But it is in Miss Maudie that we have a most remarkable woman. When her house is burnt up, she replies to Jem with robust optimism: 'Always wanted a smaller house, Jem Finch . . . Just think, I'll have more room for my azaleas now.' When the whole of Maycomb is madly excited over Tom's trial, without ever realising that it was not so much Tom as the white world on trial, Miss Maudie does not lose her head: 'I am not. 'Tis morbid watching a poor devil on trial for his life. Look at all those folks, it's like a Roman carnival.' When children put all sorts of queer questions about Arthur Radley, she replies pat:

> Stephanie Crawford even told me, once she woke up in the middle of the night and found him looking in the window at her. I said what did you do, Stephanie, move over in the bed and make room for him? That shut her up awhile.'

She tells the Finch children:

'You are too young to understand it . . . but sometimes the Bible
in the hand of one man is worse than a whiskey bottle in the hand
—oh, of your father.'

And here is the heart of the matter—the dichotomy between appearance and reality. Things are not what they seem. Both Arthur Radley and
Tom Robinson, who are punished for no crimes they ever committed, are the
representatives of all innocent victims. In fact, Radley stitching Jem's pants
torn during the children's pranks against himself, leaving gifts for the children in the <u>tree hole</u>, throwing a <u>blanket round Scout</u> while she stood shiv-
ering in a dark, cold night watching the house on fire, and finally saving
children's lives from the fatal attack of Bob Ewell, is more human than most
of the Maycomb fold. He is not the blood-thirsty devil as pictured in the
popular fantasy. And so is Tom, who was driven only by compassion to
respond to Mayella's request for help. She had assaulted him. There was no
rape. But in the court Bob Ewell shamelessly 'stood up and pointed his finger
at Tom Robinson: "I see that black nigger yonder ruttin' on my Mayella."'
Ewell and evil are almost homophones. They are filthy parasites, a blot on
society. This shows how culture has nothing to do with colour. The novelist's
moral and emotional identification with the whole problem is so great that
the verdict of the trial upsets her, too. For a moment she seems to be losing
her grip on the story. The characters are on the brink of losing their identity,
and the novelist, in her righteous anger, is on the point of reducing them to
mere mouthpieces. For even the children stunned by the judgment fumble
for words, and for a while the narrative is in danger of getting lost in the
doldrums of discussion—dull, heavy, futile. This can be understood in the
context of her having patterned the story after the model of a morality play
with a distinct line of demarcation between good and evil, right and wrong,
beautiful and ugly. Like Ewell, Cunnigham, too, betrays his character
through connotation. The finch, the family name of Atticus, means a song-
bird like the mockingbird. It is the Finch family that pits itself against evil in
defence of good. Jem Calways (sounds like Gem) and Scout are names that
do not fail to evoke a sense of value and selfless service, whereas Jean, which
is a variation of Joan, distantly clicks into our memory that angelical girl,
Joan of Arc, battling for a great cause.

To Kill a Mockingbird is a regional novel. Like Jane Austen, who does
not care to go beyond the district of Bath, or Thomas Hardy who hardly, if
ever, takes his story out of the confines of Wessex, Harper Lee sticks to
Maycomb in Alabama. The small world assumes a macrocosmic dimension

and expands into immensity, holding an epic canvas against which is enacted a movingly human drama of the jostling worlds—of children and adults, of innocence and experience, of kindness and cruelty, of love and hatred, of humour and pathos, and above all of appearance and reality—all taking the reader to the root of human behaviour. Time does not have a stop in Harper Lee's world, but it moves on lazily. The cycle of seasons keeps on turning with the ever-returning summer, and life in Maycomb, 'a tired old town', flows on in all its splendour and ugliness, joys and sorrows. Harper Lee, in her firm determination to keep away from the contemporary trend of experimentation without ever succumbing to the lure of following the footsteps of novelists like Hemingway and Faulkner, returns to the nineteenth century tradition of the well-made novel with immense facility. If she at all betrays any influence, it is from the past rather than the present—Jane Austen's morality and regionalism, Mark Twain's blending of humour and pathos in the jostling worlds, Dickens's humanitarianism and characterisation, Harriet Stowe's sentimental concern for the coloured folk. If by modernism we mean whatever that is anti-traditional, Harper Lee is not a modern, though a contemporary novelist. The contemporaneity of *To Kill a Mockingbird* is incidental, its universality essential. She tells the story with astonishing zest and yet a leisureliness characteristic of the past age. For instance, about a century divides *To Kill a Mockingbird* from Harriet Stowe's *Uncle Tom's Cabin* but there is no fundamental difference either about the content or the technique of the novels. In both we see an astonishing streak of sentimentality, an irresistible love of melodrama and the same age-old pity for the underdog. But Harper Lee has an unusual intensity of imagination which creates a world more living than the one in which we live, so very solid, so easily recognisable. It all looks so effortless, so very uncontrived. But it is painful to see the way the harsh realities impinge mercilessly on the juvenile world of innocence. Harper Lee has an intense ethical bias and there is about the novel a definite moral fervour.

The novelist, in an unmistakable way, has viewed one of the most fundamental human problems with the essentially Christian terms of reference, and we see emerging from the novel a definite moral pattern embodying a scale of values. As we notice the instinctive humanising of the world of things we are also impressed by the way Harper Lee can reconcile art and morality. For *To Kill a Mockingbird* is not a work of propaganda, it is a work of art, not without a tragic view of life. The novelist has been able to combine humour and pathos in an astonishing way. But comedy and tragedy are, in the final analysis, two sides of the same coin. The novel bubbling with life and overflowing with human emotions is not without a tragic pattern involving a contest between good and evil. Atticus in his failure to defend the

Negro victim, eventually hunted down while scaling the wall in quest of freedom, the innocent victim, and Arthur Boo, who is endowed with tender human emotions and compassion, but is nearly buried alive in the Radley House, which is a veritable sepulchre, simply because his father loved to wallow in the vanity fair, and the suffering Finch children, they all intensify the sense of waste involved in the eternal conflict. 'The hero of a tragedy,' observes Freud in *Totem and Taboo*, 'had to suffer; this is today still the essential content of a tragedy.' By that norm, *To Kill a Mockingbird* could be seen to hover on the frontier of a near-tragedy. The tragic mode is no longer a monopoly of the theatre. Like the epic that precedes it, the novel that succeeds it, too, can easily order itself into a comic or a tragic pattern. . . . *To Kill a Mockingbird* has the unity of place and action that should satisfy an Aristotle although there is no authority of the invisible here as in a Greek tragedy. With Atticus and his family at the narrative centre standing like a rock in a troubled sea of cruelty, hatred and injustice, we have an imitation of an action which is noble and of a certain magnitude. And the story, that is closed off on the melancholy note of the failure of good, also is not without its poetic justice through the nemesis that destroys the villain out to kill the Finch children. In fact, twice before the final catastrophe the story seems to be verging on its end. The first probable terminal is chapter twenty-one, when Tom is convicted and sentenced; the second is chapter twenty-six, when Tom is shot dead—not killed but set free from the coils of life, as it were—and there is nothing really left. But the novelist wants to bring the story to a rounded-off moral end. Like a symphony it starts off on a new movement after touching the lowest, almost inaudible key, and we have the crescendo of its finale. Here is exploration, or at least an honest attempt at exploration, of the whole truth which is lost in the polarities of life. But Harper Lee who lets us hear in the novel the 'still, sad music of humanity' is immensely sentimental. Her love for melodrama is inexhaustible. Hence, although her view of human life is tragic, the treatment is sentimental, even melodramatic. However, though not a tragedy, it is since *Uncle Tom's Cabin* one of the most effective expressions of the voice of protest against the injustice to the Negro in the white world. Without militant championship of 'native sons' writing in a spirit of commitment, here is a woman novelist transmuting the raw material of the Negro predicament aesthetically. . . . As we read *To Kill a Mockingbird*, a thesis novel, we notice an unfailing moral order arising out of the flux of experience which is the evolution of human consciousness elaborated through the structure of events, without ever raising the age-old problem of art and morality. There is a complete cohesion of art and morality. And therein lies the novelist's success. She is a remarkable story-teller. The reader just glides through the novel abounding in humour and pathos, hopes and fears, love and hatred, humanity and brutality—all affording him a memorable human experience of journeying through sunshine and rain at once. *To Kill a Mockingbird* is indeed a criticism of life and that, too, a most disturbing criticism, but we hardly feel any tension between the novelist's creativity and social criticism and the tale of heroic struggle lingers in our memory as an unforgettable experience while its locale, Maycomb County—'Ad Astra per Aspera: from mud to the stars'— stretches itself beyond our everyday horizon as an old familiar world.

WILLIAM T. GOING

Store and Mockingbird:
Two Pulitzer Novels about Alabama

One of the things about [T. S.] Stribling that disturbed Robert Penn Warren in 1934 when he was writing about the new Pulitzer Prize winner was that the author "has never been interested in the dramatic possibilities of a superior white man brought into conflict with his native environment," a matter that has challenged many serious Southern novelists like William Faulkner and Caroline Gordon. A quarter of a century later Miss Lee has done precisely that for the Alabama scene [in *To Kill a Mockingbird*]. Even though it is usually easier to write about the spectacular, wicked man, Miss Lee has chosen the more difficult task of writing about the quiet, good man. Other novelists have been concerned with this type of man—the thoughtful, well-educated Southerner at quiet odds with his environment like the minor character Gavin Stevens in Faulkner's *Intruder in the Dust*. But Miss Lee has made him the central figure and hero of her novel and succeeded at the same time in writing an exciting and significant story.

The epigraph from Charles Lamb—"Lawyers, I suppose, were once children"—indicates the two aspects of *Mockingbird*, childhood and the law. The plot can be simply stated: Atticus Finch, one of Maycomb's leading attorneys, is the court-appointed defender of Tom Robinson, accused of raping Mayella Ewell, a daughter of the town's notorious poor white-trash family. In this struggle he is unsuccessful—at least the all-white jury finds

From *Essays on Alabama Literature*. © 1975 by William T. Going.

Tom guilty, and he is killed escaping from prison before Atticus can gain a hearing on the appeal. But to a certain extent the case is not altogether lost; certain precedents have been set. Instead of a young lawyer who defends only for the record's sake Judge Taylor appoints a distinguished lawyer who chooses to fight obvious lies and racial hatred so that he and his children— and ultimately Maycomb itself—can remain honest and honorable people. No one except Atticus Finch ever kept a jury out so long on a case involving a Negro. And in the process of the trial Atticus's children have matured in the right way—at least in his eyes.

The struggle of the children toward maturity, however, occupies more space than Atticus's struggle to free Tom, the central episode. Through their escapades and subsequent entanglements with their father and neighbors like Miss Maudie Atkinson, Mrs. Henry Lafayette Dubose, and particularly the legends about Boo Radley, the town's boogie man, Jem and Scout learn what it means to come to man's estate. In Part I, an evocation of the happy days of summer play, the process is begun. With their friend Dill Harris from Meridian they enact the weird stories about Boo Radley—how he sits in his shuttered house all day and wanders about in the shadows of night looking in people's windows, how he once drove the scissors into his father's leg, how as a not-too-bright adolescent he had terrorized the county with a "gang" from Old Sarum. Might he even be dead in that solemn, silent house, the children wonder. Miss Maudie gives, as always, a forthright answer to that question: "I know he's alive, Jean Louise, because I haven't seen him carried out yet." Although Atticus forbids these "Boo Radley" games, the children go on playing. . . .

In the midst of these juvenile Gothic masques the children begin to learn something about the difference between gossip and truth. When Jem tears his pants and is forced to leave them behind on the wire fence during their night expedition to peek through the Radleys' shutters, he later finds them crudely mended, pressed, and hanging over the fence. When Miss Maudie's house burns during a cold night, all the neighborhood turns out to help and to watch. Scout, who is told to come no closer than the Radleys' gate, discovers that during the confusion a blanket has been thrown round her shoulders. Jem realizes that this thoughtful act was not performed by Mr. or Mrs. Radley, who have long been dead, and he saw Mr. Nathan, Boo's brother and "jailer," helping haul out Miss Maudie's mattress. It could have been only Boo.

One of the most interesting features of *Mockingbird* is the skill with which Miss Lee weaves these two struggles about childhood and the law together into one thematic idea. . . . [She] does a neat workmanlike job of dovetailing her plots. When Scout attends her first day at school, the morning session is devoted to explaining the Cunningham family to Miss Caroline so that she will understand why she must not lend Walter any lunch money. The Cunninghams are poor but proud. When the Sunday night lynching party arrives at the jail, it is Jem and Scout, who, having slipped off from home, see their father calmly reading a newspaper by the light at the jail door, sitting in one of his office chairs. Hiding in the doorway of the Jitney Jungle, Scout rushes forward in time to disconcert the Cunningham mob by asking innocent questions about Walter, her classmate—her father had always taught her to talk to folks about the things that would interest them.

The afternoon session of Scout's first day at school had been taken up with Burris Ewell and his dirt and defiance of Miss Caroline. It is Burris's father who brings the charge of rape against Tom Robinson.

This neatness that makes for economy of character portrayal is successful when it avoids the appearance of too convenient coincidental circumstances—a fault that *Mockingbird* does not entirely escape. But in the more important aspect of thematic development the novel is successful. Carson McCullers and Truman Capote have written with insight about Southern childhood, and William Faulkner has traced the legal and moral injustices done the Negro just as Eudora Welty has underlined the quiet patience of the Negro's acceptance of his bleak world. Harper Lee has united these two concepts into the image of a little child—schooled in basic decencies by her father even though "ladylike" manners of the superficial sort that Aunt Alexandra admires are sometimes lacking—who turns the tide to stop the Sunday night lynching. After the trial when Jem cannot comprehend the injustice done Tom Robinson by the jury, he asks his father, "How could they do it, how could they?" Atticus replies, "I don't know, but they did it. They've done it before and they did it tonight and they'll do it again and when they do it—seems that only the children weep."

Almost all readers will agree that the first two-thirds of *Mockingbird* is excellent fiction; the difference of opinion will probably turn upon the events after the trial. The major incident here is the school pageant about the history of Maycomb County as written by Mrs. Merriweather; the performance is the town's attempt at "organized activity" on Halloween. On their way home from the pageant, Ewell attacks the Finch children to get even with Atticus for making him appear a complete and guilty fool at Tom's trial. Scout is saved from the knife by her wire costume representing a Maycomb County ham; Jem receives a painful broken arm. And Ewell is killed with his own knife by Boo Radley, who again lurks opportunely in the shadows. Later that night after visits from the doctor and the sheriff when Scout is allowed to walk home with Mr. Arthur, she stands for a moment on the Radley porch seeing the knothole in the tree where Boo had once left them pitiful little presents of chewing gum and Indianhead pennies. She half realizes as a child of nine, and now as an adult she more fully realizes, what their childish antics must have meant to a lonely, "imprisoned," mentally limited man like Mr. Arthur, and she recalls her father's word to Jem that "you never really know a man until you stand in his shoes and walk around in them. Just standing on the Radley porch was enough."

Thematically the aftermath of the injustice done Tom and the growing up of a boy and girl are brought together in the Halloween episode. The structural problem of joining Boo Radley and Tom Robinson into some sort of juxtaposition is solved, but the slapstick comedy of the school pageant and the grotesque coincidental tragedy and subsequent salvation are perilously close to the verge of melodrama. . . . To keep this section of *Mockingbird* from seeming altogether an anticlimax to the trial of Tom, it should at least have been denominated Part III. Then the story would have been set off into its three components of School and Summer Play, Tom Robinson's Trial, and Halloween Masquerade. Such a device would distribute the thirty-one chapters into the equal grouping of Miss Lee's apparent planning, and at the same time it would not force the Halloween tragi-comedy to seem quite so close to the climactic trial.

It is strange that the structural *forte* of *Mockingbird*, the point of view of the telling, is either misunderstood or misinterpreted by most of the initial reviewers of the novel. Phoebe Adams in the *Atlantic Monthly* calls it "frankly and completely impossible, being told in the first person by a six-year-old girl with the prose and style of a well-educated adult." Richard Sullivan in the *Chicago Tribune* is puzzled and only half understands: "The unaffected young narrator uses adult language to render the matter she deals with, but the point of view is cunningly restricted to that of a perceptive, independent child, who doesn't always understand fully what's happening, but who conveys completely, by implication, the weight and burden of the story." [These reviews are excerpted in CLC, Vol. 12.] More careful reviewers like Granville Hicks in the *Saturday Review* [see excerpt above] and F. H. Lyell in the *New York Times* [see also CL C, Vol. 12] are more perceptive. The latter states the matter neatly: "Scout is the narrator, reflecting in maturity on childhood events of the mid-Thirties."

Maycomb and the South, then, are all seen through the eyes of Jean Louise, who speaks from the mature and witty vantage of an older woman recalling her father as well as her brother and their childhood days. This method is managed with so little ado that the average reader slips well into the story before he realizes that the best evidence that Atticus has reared an intellectually sophisticated daughter is that she remembers her formative years in significant detail and then narrates them with charm and wisdom.

She has become the good daughter of a good man, who never let his children know what an expert marksman he was until he was forced to kill a mad dog on their street. Atticus did not like to shoot for the mere sport of it lest he kill a mockingbird like Tom Robinson or Boo Radley; and mockingbirds must be protected for their songs' sake.

This modification of a Jamesian technique of allowing the story to be seen only through the eyes of a main character but to be understood by the omniscient intelligence of Henry James is here exploited to bold advantage. The reader comes to learn the true meaning of Maycomb through the eyes of a child who now recollects with the wisdom of maturity. Along with Scout and Jem we may at first be puzzled why Atticus insists that Jem read every afternoon to old Mrs. Henry Lafayette Dubose in atonement for his cutting the tops off her camellia bushes after she taunted him about his father's being "no better than the niggers and trash he works for." But we soon learn with Scout that Atticus believed Jem would become aware of the real meaning of courage when he was forced to aid a dying old woman in breaking the narcotic habit she abhorred.

Jean Louise's evolving perception of the social milieu in her home town as she grows up in it and as she recalls her own growing up involves the reader in an understanding of the various strata of Maycomb society and its Southern significance. After Jem has brooded about the trial, he explains to Scout that

> "There's four kinds of folks in the world. There's the ordinary kind like us and the neighbors, there's the kind like the Cunninghams out in the woods, the kind like the Ewells down at the dump, and the Negroes."
>
> "What about the Chinese, and the Cajuns down yonder in Baldwin County?"
>
> "I mean in Maycomb County. The thing about it is, our kind of folks don't like the Cunninghams and the Cunninghams don't like the Ewells, and the Ewells hate and despise the colored folks."
>
> I told Jem if that was so, then why didn't Tom's jury, made up of folks like the Cunninghams, acquit Tom to spite the Ewells?

After considerable debate Scout concludes, "New, Jem, I think there's just one kind of folks. Folks."

This naively sophisticated sociological rationalization is far more valid and persuasive in its two-pronged approach. As mature readers we realize its mature validity; as observers of children we delight in their alert reactions to the unfolding events. The convolutions of the "mind of Henry James" have given way to the immediacy and pithy wisdom of Jean Louise's first-person narration.

Though Miss Lee may not have solved all her problems of style in the dual approach of child eyes and mature heart, *Mockingbird* demonstrates the powerful effect and economy of a well-conceived point of view. . . .

Miss Lee, in a sense, has actually revealed more of Alabama history from the Simon Finches of old Saint Stephens to distrusted Republicans like the Misses Barber from Clanton than does Stribling in [*The Store*], his much longer historical novel. The spirit of history is as important as the events of history, and Miss Lee presents Miss Caroline as an outsider from Winston County because she represents to this Maycomb community what every South Alabama child knew about north Alabama: a place "full of Liquor Interests, Big Mules, steel companies, Republicans, professors, and other persons of no background." Miss Lee has mastered an eclectic technique of a meaningful point of view along with validity of idea and freshness of mate-rial. She echoes Faulkner in her deep concern for the inchoate tragedy of the South, and like him she is not afraid to pursue the Gothic shadows of Edgar Allan Poe. But her eclecticism is her own: she has told a story of racial injus-tice from the point of view of thoughtful children with "open, unprejudiced, well-furnished minds of their own," as the *New York Times* has phrased it. And in Atticus Finch she has created the most memorable portrait in recent fiction of the just and equitable Southern liberal.

CLAUDIA DURST JOHNSON

The Secret Courts of Men's Hearts:
Code and Law in Harper Lee's To Kill a Mockingbird

In Harper Lee's *To Kill a Mockingbird*, Atticus Finch's final hope in the defense of his black client accused of rape is that he may strike a favorable response in his summation to the south Alabama jury by appealing to the official legal code of the United States:

> "There is one way in this country in which all men are created equal—there is one human institution that makes a pauper the equal of a Rockefeller, the stupid man the equal of an Einstein, and the ignorant man the equal of any college president. That institution, gentlemen, is a court. It can be the Supreme Court of the United States or the humblest J. P. court in the land, or this honorable court which you serve. Our courts have their faults, as does any human institution, but in this country our courts are the great levelers, and in our courts all men are created equal."

Atticus is grieved by what he cannot at this moment say without jeopardizing his case, that the law of the land is one thing and "the secret court of men's hearts" quite another. *To Kill A Mockingbird* presents the argument that the forces that motivate society are not consonant with the democratic ideals embedded in its legal system and that the disjunction between the codes men

---

From *Studies in American Fiction* 19:2 (Autumn 1991). © 1991 by Northeastern University.

and women profess and those they live by threatens to unravel individual lives as well as the social fabric. The novel is set in the 1930s, was written in the late 1950s, periods when the South, Alabama particularly, was a case study of that proposition. The three years at the end of the 1950s, when the novel was written, form one of the most turbulent periods of race relations in a state with a turbulent history, a time when a long-standing relationship between blacks and whites, maintained in refutation of the spirit of American democracy, was being tested in the courts. The novel reveals a time when rulings handed down from "the secret courts of men's hearts" became the laws they lived by openly, in defiance not only of all reason but of the laws they professed to have gone to war to uphold.

The historical context of the novel is replete with actual court cases bearing on the complex issues of constitutional and personal law. The notorious precursor to Alabama's legal battles of the fifties was the Scottsboro case of the 1930s. It is significant that only a few years before the setting of Lee's novel (1933 to 1935) about a black man accused of raping a white woman who had made sexual advances toward him, nine black men were charged in a notorious trial with raping two white women "of easy virtue." Numerous celebrated legal battles arising from the Scottsboro trial were reported in the Southern and Northern press during those years when Scout, the thinly-veiled autobiographical protagonist of the novel, was precociously reading *The Montgomery Advertiser*, *The Mobile Register*, and *Time*. Doubtless, the young Nell Harper Lee, daughter of a moderate Southern attorney who had encouraged her precocity in legal matters, consciously or unconsciously absorbed for later literary use the circumstances and arguments surrounding the numerous Scottsboro trials of her youth in the thirties. In the summer of 1935, Atticus and his son Jem have an extended discussion about the composition of juries after an all-male, all-white jury convicts Atticus' client, Tom Robinson, of rape. On April 2, 1935, the front page of *The Montgomery Advertiser* reported that new trials had been ordered by the Supreme Court for two of the Scottsboro "boys," Clarence Norris and Haywood Patterson, on the grounds that no blacks had served on their juries. The South's dual system of justice is freely acknowledged in the *Advertiser's* editorial: blacks are not excluded from juries technically or legally, the editors claim, but "in common practice they are, of course."

It is reasonable to believe that the issues in *To Kill a Mockingbird* were shaped by the 1950s when it was written as well as the 1930s chosen for its setting. The initiating circumstance in the South's history of that period was the 1954 Supreme Court ruling that school segregation was unconstitutional. In 1955, only months before Harper Lee began committing her fiction to paper, two of the most startling events in Alabama history had jarred the state, wrenching it irreversibly in a radically different direction. The central figures in both events were black women: Rosa Parks, who on November 30, 1955, refused to give up her bus seat to a white passenger; and Autherine Lucy, who, on February 3, 1956, presented herself for registration in the racially segregated University of Alabama where Harper Lee had been enrolled as a student of law a decade earlier.

From the opening pages of the novel, trappings of plot and dialogue direct the reader to the complexities of law, Southern style. The novel is prefaced with a line from Charles Lamb, "Lawyers, I suppose were children once," an inscription in reference to both of Atticus Finch's children who presumably grow up to be lawyers. The lines obviously refer to his son, Jem, who, the family understands, wants to be a lawyer like his father and who, as a child, is able to follow with greater interest and acumen than most adults the nuances of a trial that is the central event of the novel. Less obviously, the lines from Lamb also refer to Atticus' daughter-narrator, taunted by the missionary ladies (because she attended the rape trial) for wanting to grow up to be a lawyer. The reader is not told if the narrator is a practicing attorney when she tells the story, but one does recognize her to be a student of the law in the broadest sense. The novel itself is, in part, her convincing brief for her father's sainthood, a reversal of the usual American cliché of adolescent patricide. That Lee's readers, who are in a sense her jury, so readily render a decision in Atticus' favor, closing the case as it were, may in some way account for the subsequent silence of this authorial voice.

Relationships in the novel are often presented as legal arrangements. The cement of the fictional town of Maycomb, a community whose "primary reason for existence was government," is shown to be its formal and informal law: entailments (to which poor but honest Mr. Cunningham falls victim), compromises (between Scout and Atticus over her reading and going to school), state legislative bills (introduced by Atticus, a legislator), treaties (between the Finch children and their neighbor, Miss Maudie, over her azaleas), truancy laws (that the poor and lawless Ewell children, but not Scout, are allowed to break), hunting and trapping laws (violated by Bob Ewell), and bending the law (an issue on which the novel closes). The pervasiveness of legal allusions extends even to their maid Calpurnia, the Finch children's surrogate mother, who has been taught to read and teaches her son to read, using Blackstone's *Commentaries*.

The major subplots arise from breaches in the law: the ancient story of the arrest of the Finches' reclusive neighbor, Boo Radley, for disorderly conduct, and his later attack on his father, the children's trespassing on Radley property, the attempted lynching of the black prisoner, Tom Robinson, the alleged rape of Mayella Ewell, and the assault and murder that conclude the novel.

The narrator frequently presents legalistic community relationships by negation, portraying outlaws and outcasts, both sympathetic and unsympathetic, who deliberately or inadvertently violate community codes. Of course, Scout is herself an outlaw, an observation that ladies in the area, especially her Aunt Alexandra, had made from the moment Atticus was left alone to raise her and Jem with only the help of a black woman. Scout discovers her own oddity in first grade when her teacher scolds her for having already learned to read. She drags home from school, "weary from the day's crimes." So Scout is, understandably, immediately drawn to Dill, an outcast from a broken family that scolds him for "not being a boy." Together, the three children, Scout, her brother, Jem, and Dill, are attracted to nightwalkers, outlaws in truth (Boo Radley) and in fiction (Dracula). In addition to the Radleys, other eccentric neighbors who influence their lives, because in varying degrees they skirt accepted codes of behavior, are Miss Maudie, who is railed at by foot-washing Baptists for her azaleas, their blooms testimonies to her excessive love of the natural world, and Mrs. Dubose, an addict of morphine. Outside the court house, Scout is introduced to Dolphus Raymond, a man who has violated the southern code by preferring the company of blacks to whites, and has "'got a colored woman and all sorts of mixed chillun.'" The "mixed chillun" are a new concept for Scout. She can empathize with their being "just in-betweens, don't belong anywhere." The trial brings together the victims and villains of both written and subterranean laws. Tom Robinson broke a code, no less powerful because unexpressed, by feeling sorry for a white woman. Mayella Ewell violated an equally powerful unwritten code by kissing a black man. Of her, Atticus says, "'no code mattered to her before she broke it.'" The villainy of her father, Bob Ewell, arises from his unwillingness to be governed by any law, either internal or external; his crimes run from the petty breaking of hunting and truancy laws to incest and attempted murder. His counterpart in moral chaos on an international scale is Adolph Hitler.

Obviously the thematic scope of *To Kill a Mockingbird* goes beyond the narrow limits of written laws. It is rather a study of the law in its broadest sense: familial, communal, and regional codes; those of the drawing room and the school yard; those written and unwritten; some that lie beneath the surface in dark contradiction of established law. Although its attorney hero, Atticus Finch, and the son that will follow in his footsteps, maintain a simple Christ-like goodness and wisdom in the memory of the narrator, what she unfolds, in a story turning on her father and brother, is neither simple nor conclusive, for the codes that motivate people in this Alabama community promote destruction as often as they prevent it.

A drama founded on Maycomb's legal and social codes, extraordinarily complex for such a tiny community, is played out not on just one but several different stages; one might even say "courtrooms." The primary ones—the Finch house, the courthouse, the schoolhouse, and the Ewell house—are little communities unto themselves, each with its own scheme of relationships, often, like the community of Maycomb as a whole, with a hidden code as well as an open one and largely based on physical difference (gender, race, and age) as well as class.

The novel is a study of how Jem and Scout begin to perceive the complexity of social codes and how the configuration of relationships dictated by or set off by those codes fails or nurtures the inhabitants of these small worlds. In the aftermath of the court case, which is a moral victory and legal defeat for their father, Jem and Scout discuss the heart of the matter, the postlapsarian fragmentation of the human community. Neither Scout nor Jem can account for what they have begun to observe, society's division of the human family into hostile camps. Scout, never able to get a satisfactory answer from Aunt Alexandra, for whom class, race, and gender are exclusionary categories, speculates momentarily that these isolating distinctions have something to do with whether a group likes fiddle music and pot liquor. Scout rejects Jem's theory, at which he has arrived after long deliberation, that the key is literacy: "'Naw, Jem, I think there's just one kind of folks. Folks.'" Scout's magnanimity arises naturally from her experience as a child in the house of Atticus Finch, their growing up coinciding with their exposure to the complex weave of codes in the social fabric of Maycomb. The children are first shaped by an Eden where love, truth, and wholeness have brought the household to a highly refined moral plane. As Tom Robinson's trial proceeds, the children become gradually aware of a world in sharp contrast to the one they had known. Bob Ewell is the antithesis of Atticus. As his realm surfaces, they become aware that perverse hidden codes and lawlessness, generally associated with the worst of bigotry and ignorance in a place called Old Sarum, have surfaced in the actions of the jury. Scout's suspicion of a dark underside of the community, first uncovered in the conviction of Tom, is alarmingly and unconsciously confirmed by Aunt Alexandra and the missionary society. In short, Old Sarum, the habitation of poor, hard-drinking, lynch-prone dirt farmers on the edge of town, has invaded polite Maycomb.

Scout's realization of the difference between Maycomb's idealistic law and its unacknowledged but real laws begins in a setting where this disjunction had not earlier existed, where the saint-like Atticus bestowed a benevolent order on the Finch household by his example. The chief lesson he had taught his children was to make every effort to walk in the shoes of other people in order to understand them. He is a peacemaker, refusing to hunt or carry arms, insisting that his children turn the other cheek rather than resort to violence against man or beast. It is wrong, he tells Scout, to hate anybody, even Hitler. Atticus' saintliness has nothing to do with cowardice or impotence. He is a savior, capable of facing a mad dog and a lynch mob. He is, Miss Maudie tells Jem, "'born to do our unpleasant jobs for us.'" His brother, recognizing a holy agony in Atticus' description of the impending trial, is led to respond: "'Let this cup pass from you, eh?'" Further, in explaining true courage to Jem and Scout, Atticus defines a tragic hero, which, as it turns out, is a description of his own role in the case of Tom Robinson: "'It's when you know you're licked before you begin but you begin anyway and you see it through no matter what. You rarely win, but sometimes you do.'" Atticus' heroism is a quality that Maycomb's black population fully recognize. In the most carefully crafted and emotionally packed moment of the novel, as Atticus is leaving the courtroom after his defeat, simultaneously Scout realizes that all the spectators in the balcony are standing and is urged to her feet by the black preacher: " 'Miss Jean Louise, stand up. Your father's passin.'"

A house ordered by the laws of such a man might be expected to be as nurturing as it is eccentric. It is at one and the same time the most innocent and the most civilized of countries. Indeed as a family, the Finches seem to have moved upward through the various stages of civilization represented in the community. In their past is racial persecution (their slaveholding founder), incest (Atticus teases Alexandra, "'would you say the Finches have an Incestuous Streak?'"), and madness (Cousin Joshua St. Clair, long before institutionalized in Tuscaloosa). While most of Maycomb is still in a primordial stage, the higher evolution of Atticus is apparent in his achievement of a code that rises above hate, egocentricity, and madness. Bigotry has been superceded by a higher law: people are to be regarded as individuals, human beings, not as dehumanized types. This is the crux of his argument at trial: "'You know the truth, and the truth is this: some Negroes lie, some Negroes are immoral, some Negro men are not to be trusted around women—black or white. But this is a truth that applies to the human race and to no particular race of men'" (p. 207). And it is a position that he argues outside the courtroom as well. About the lynch mob he says: "'A mob's always made up of people, no matter what. Mr. Cunningham was part of a mob last night, but he was still a man.'"

One of the keys to the benevolence of Atticus' law is that it blurs the lines that mark out gender and race, diminishing the superficial barriers thrown up to hamper and privilege. In the novel, the limitations of gender run parallel to the more obvious limitations of race. Scout, whose very nickname is boyish, is allowed to be herself, an adventurous tomboy whose customary attire is overalls, who rarely dons a skirt, who plays and fights with boys and is given a gun instead of a doll for Christmas. Even customs in recognition of age are often disregarded here. The children call Atticus by his first name, and Scout learns to read before she is "supposed to." The same can be said of class barriers. Walter Cunningham, a dirt-poor Old Sarum child outside their social class, is invited home to lunch and treated as an honored guest.

The children are taught to look and reach outward. Rising above self-protection and exclusion, they embrace difference. That they want to know about people unlike themselves is part of the explanation for their obsession with Boo Radley and with Scout's wish to visit black Calpurnia's house: "I was curious, interested; I wanted to be her 'company,' to see how she lived, who her friends were."

Of all the societies that the children will ever encounter, this one is the most whole, therefore the most sane. Heart and head rule in harmony, inner and outer laws work in tandem, for there are no hidden agendas, no double standards, no dark secrets here. What Atticus has to say about race he will say in front of Calpurnia. When a child asks him something, he believes in answering truthfully. What Atticus preaches, he also practices: "'I can't live one way in town and another way in my own house.'" It is with this wholeness of spirit that Atticus confronts the madness, just as he does a rabid dog in the street. But Atticus' code is a far remove from the realities of Maycomb, Alabama, as Jem senses after Tom Robinson's conviction: "'It's like bein' a caterpillar in a cocoon, that's what it is,' he said. 'Like somethin' asleep wrapped up in a warm place. I always thought Maycomb folks were the best folks in the world, least that's what they seemed like.'"

The agents that destroy the children's Eden, in which benevolent laws are blind to artificial distinctions, are the citizens of Old Sarum and Bob Ewell, whose house is an inversion of Atticus' house. Certain parallels between the two households invite contrast: both Scout and Mayella Ewell are without biological mothers and without girlfriends. Scout never mentions another young girl her age at school or at play and is even gradually being excluded from the companionship of Jem and Dill. Mayella seems not even to understand the concept of friendship, male or female. Both girls are more vulnerable in that their fathers are consequently accorded more power for good or evil than they would have had otherwise. Ewell and Atticus are pointedly opposite, however. Ewell hunts even out of season; Atticus refuses to hunt at all. Ewell takes his children from school, while Atticus will not allow the dissatisfied Scout to be a truant. Ewell obviously beats Mayella viciously; Atticus has "never laid a hand" on his children. Atticus is selfless in his love for Scout; Ewell is self-gratifying in his sexual abuse of Mayella. In sum, violence has been superceded in Atticus' life by love and laws; the violence of Ewell's life is untempered by sanity.

Jem, in particular, is traumatized because the law in theory had been sacred to him, but in practice it is mendacious, uncovering a powerful, concealed code at work in complete contradiction to written law. The democratic ideal is stated by Atticus in his summation: " 'In this country our courts are the great levelers, and in our courts all men are created equal.'" It is a sentiment repeated by Scout at school: democracy, she parrots, means "'equal rights for all, special privileges for none.'" However, even the apparatus of the court plainly countermands the official line. Only Negroes, not white men, are remanded to Maycomb's jail. In the court room, black men and women are restricted to the balcony. No women and no blacks serve on juries. But more pernicious than any of these contradictions is the existence, as the narrator puts it, of "the secret court of men's hearts" where madness makes a mockery of equality before the law. Society officially expects Atticus, as a court appointed lawyer, to defend Tom Robinson, but in the secret court of society's heart Atticus is faulted for doing the job it has given him: "'Lemme tell you somethin' now, Billy,' a third said, 'you know the court appointed him to defend this nigger.' 'Yeah, but Atticus aims to defend him. That's what I don't like about it.'"

Paralleling Jem's trauma in the male arena of the courthouse is Scout's enlightenment in the female arena of her aunt's missionary society. Aunt Alexandra brings with her a system of codification and segregation of the human family according to class, race, and, in Scout's case, sex. Even earlier from the Finch ancestral home, the Landing, Aunt Alexandra had presented a threat:

> Aunt Alexandra was fanatical on the subject of my attire. I could
> not possibly hope to be a lady if I wore breeches; when I could
> do nothing in a dress, she said I wasn't supposed to be doing
> things that required pants. Aunt Alexandra's vision of my deport-
> ment involved playing with small stoves, tea sets, and wearing the
> Add-A-Pearl necklace she gave me when I was born.

When Aunt Alexandra invades the Finch house in Maycomb as a "feminine influence," Scout feels "a pink cotton penitentiary closing in on me." Aunt Alexandra brings with her a code that delineates very narrowly ladies and gentlemen, black and white people, "good" families and trash. She files them in their proper, neat, separate boxes. Fearing contamination, she forbids Scout to visit Calpurnia's house or to invite Walter Cunningham to the Finch home again. Scout concludes that "Aunt Alexandra fitted into the world of Maycomb like a hand into a glove, but never into the world of Jem and me."

The larger society into which families, church, school, and local government fit is characterized by many of the Finches' neighbors and friends in general and the missionary society in particular, longtime residents in the mainstream of the community. The perniciousness of this society arises from its system of dual, contradictory codes. Superficially the missionary ladies abide by the customs of gentility in "a world, where on its surface fragrant ladies rocked slowly, fanned gently, and drank cool water." They also, superficially, respond to the dictates of their religion by gathering together on errands of Christian charity. The official topic of discussion on one afternoon after Tom Robinson's trial is the far-flung Mrundas, a primitive tribe infected with yaws and earworms and, the ladies fear, possessed of no sense of family, "'the poverty . . . the darkness . . . the immorality . . .'" Their expression of sympathy for the Mrundas is a charitable, public formality. It is apparent, however, in a scene as primitive and tribal in its way as the Mrundas could ever be, that a greater countermanding force lies beneath the surface, one neither Christlike nor charitable nor gentle. Espousals to the contrary, it is this dark code that actually governs their lives. They cuttingly and cruelly censure Atticus in his own house and in the presence of his nine-year-old daughter and his sister, their hostess. The missionary ladies can safely exclude blacks from the sisterhood of the human race by failing to view them as other than types, establishing with heart and mind a segregation more pernicious than any system maintained by law. Mrs. Merryweather, the most prominent member of the society, who has devoted herself to bringing the word of Christ to the Mrundas, ironically speculates that trying to Christianize American black people may be useless. She and the other ladies are peevish and self-righteous in their plan to "convert" Tom Robinson's wife, regarding the black woman's membership in her own church as somewhat beside the point. They grudgingly agree to "forgive" her for being the widow of a black man wrongly convicted of raping a white woman. A corrective is provided by Scout who, untrained in their racial distinctions, believes, before they name Helen Robinson, that the ladies are speaking of the white woman, Mayella Ewell, who lodged the accusation against Tom Robinson.

The meeting of the missionary society undercuts Atticus' and Miss Maudie's attempts to reassure the children that Maycomb is not as bad as the jury that convicted Tom Robinson. The blind intolerance of the jury of rural, uneducated, white males does not, they had implied, characterize the larger community. The assurance given to Scout by the two adults she most respects in the world is shaken not only by the missionary society meeting but by her teacher, Mrs. Evans, who also illustrates that geographical distance makes her democratic and charitable propensities eminently easier to maintain. Mrs. Evans flies the national colors in deploring Hitler's persecution of the Jews as she writes across the blackboard in large letters, "DEMOCRACY." But outside the courthouse after Tom Robinson's conviction, Scout has glimpsed a different set of rules by which the teacher lives. Scout hears Mrs. Evans say, "it's time somebody taught 'em a lesson, they were gettin' way above themselves, an' the next thing they think they can do is marry us." Scout feels, but has not completely intellectualized, the same thing that is torturing Jem: beneath the surface of the world they belong to and must live in there lies another frightening force that threatens to unsettle it all. Just below the surface lie the poor Mrundas, Old Sarum, and Adolph Hitler.

Harper Lee doubtless could write about her fiction what Nathaniel Hawthorne wrote of *The Scarlet Letter*, that the events of those years in which the work was conceived had a decided effect on the novel itself. The trial of Tom Robinson in *To Kill a Mockingbird* represents a pattern of actual occurrences in Alabama during the late 1950s. The jury that condemned Tom was made up of ignorant and bigoted rural Old Sarum Southerners because women and blacks were "in practice" excluded from juries and because educated middle- and upper-class whites refused to jeopardize their positions by serving on juries. Atticus clarifies:

> "Our stout Maycomb citizens aren't interested, in the first place. In the second place, they're afraid. . . . Say, Mr. Link Deas had to decide the amount of damages to award, say Miss Maudie, when Miss Rachel ran over her with a car, Link wouldn't like the thought of losing either lady's business at his store, would he? So he tells Judge Taylor that he can't serve on the jury because he doesn't have anybody to keep the store while he's gone. So Judge Taylor excuses him."

This circumstance parallels events in Alabama in 1956, when, metaphorically speaking, Old Sarum and Old Hitler (as Scout's classmate insists on calling the dictator) had surfaced in white Southern society, coming in from the dark to take action while "reasonable" citizens, to protect themselves, abdicated responsibility. Throughout 1957 and 1958, for instance, newspapers reported repeated attempts, some successful, to bomb the homes and churches of black civil rights workers in Alabama, culminating in the death of four black children in a church bombing in Birmingham in 1963. Like practitioners of witchcraft, the Ku Klux Klan of the 1950s and the fictional Old Sarum and Bob Ewell of the 1930s are inversions of the religious and political principles they profess, actually and symbolically burning the cross under cover of darkness.

The policy of nonviolence practiced by Martin Luther King and his followers was not as successful as Atticus' nonviolent encounter with the Old Sarum lynch mob. In a similar real-life event, the wife of University of Alabama president O. C. Carmichael was pelted with eggs and stones when she appeared on the steps of her house to speak to a mob objecting to the admission of Autherine Lucy, one instance in a series of events that showed "the apparent triumph of mob violence over the law of the land," as Suzanne Rau Wolfe notes in *The University of Alabama: A Pictorial History*. Ironically, it is with reciprocal violence, perpetrated entirely outside the law and by a madman in darkness that the *fictional* children in *To Kill a Mockingbird* are saved while the *real* black offspring of disciples (like Atticus) of non-violence are bombed in a church. In short, in the dark hour of the novel, Atticus' higher law is an ineffective defense against Bob Ewell's chaos, as useless as facing a mad dog in the street without a gun. Only a miracle, some *deus ex machina*, in this case Boo Radley, can overcome chaos. Even a human and civilized system of law becomes at some point, and under certain circumstances, severely limited when primitive, hidden codes or lawlessness merge so powerfully. In the case of Boo Radley's killing of Bob Ewell, law is proven inadequate for another reason, because on occasion laws must be overridden for justice to be done. Circumstance must override honor; an individual human being's needs must supercede principle. Ewell's death must be reported as an accidental suicide instead of as a homicide. It is not a step that Atticus takes lightly.

> "If this thing's hushed up it'll be a simple denial to Jem of the way I've tried to raise him. . . . Jem and Scout know what happened. If they hear of me saying down town something different happened—Heck, I won't have them any more. I can't live one way in town and another way in my home."

But Atticus has always been more insistent that he and his own strong kind obey a higher law (pulling them up the evolutionary ladder) than the weak Ewells and Cunninghams. Only when he finds that it is not Jem but Boo who has killed Bob Ewell does he relent to the secrecy that will circumvent a legal hearing. For Atticus knows Boo to be "one of the least of these," as scripture delineates the earth's dispossessed, those who stand in for Christ. In a final act that secures Atticus' sainthood, he momentarily, hesitantly relinquishes for Boo Radley's sake what is more sacred to him, the code he lives by.

CLAUDIA DURST JOHNSON

Literary Analysis: Unifying Elements of To Kill a Mockingbird

Universal Themes

The success of *To Kill a Mockingbird*, one of the most frequently read novels of the last hundred years, can be attributed to its powerful, universal themes. One central theme, encompassing both Part One (which is primarily Boo Radley's story) and Part Two (which is primarily Tom Robinson's story), is that valuable lessons are learned in confronting those who are unlike ourselves and unlike those we know best—what might be called people of difference. In the story, the children must grow up, learn civilizing truths, and rise above the narrowness of the place and time in which private codes and even some legal practices contradict the idealistic principles that the community professes: "Equal rights for all, special privileges for none," as Scout says. In practice, however, equal justice was not available to Boo Radley at that turning point in his life; nor is it available to the Tom Robinsons of this world.

Within such a social climate, the children learn how citizens of their community, which is made up of different races, classes, and temperaments, interact in times of crisis. The "outsiders" in this novel are primarily represented by the unseen eccentric, Boo Radley, and by the African-American, Tom Robinson. They are clearly outside the mainstream of Maycomb society, even though they have lived in the community for as long as most

From *Understanding To Kill a Mockingbird: A Student Casebook to Issues, Sources, and Historic Documents*. © 1994 by Claudia Durst Johnson.

can remember. Because of their position in society, they are at first regarded by the children as demonic and witchlike. But in the process of maturing, the children come to embrace the outsiders among them. Even more, they come to acknowledge their kinship with the outsiders—in a sense, the outsider within themselves.

During the course of the novel, the children pass from innocence to knowledge. They begin to realize their own connection with the community's outsiders, and they observe one man's heroism in the face of community prejudice. One overarching theme of the novel—which brings Part One, the story of Boo Radley and the children, in union with Part Two, the trial of Tom Robinson—can be stated in this way: the mark of virtue, not to mention maturity and civilization, involves having the insight and courage to value human differences—people unlike ourselves and people we might label as outsiders.

In this novel the emphasis is on people of a race and culture different from that of the Finch children, but it also includes the eccentric Boo Radleys of the world who are so different from the people we are and know that they become witchlike and demonlike in the homogeneous community's consciousness. After all, difference is unsettling, even frightening. As the children learn, it takes a strong mind and a big heart to come to love Boo Radley, of whom they are at first so terrified; and it takes immense courage to defend another human being, one who is different from themselves, against community injustice borne of fear.

Certainly, as Atticus says in his final summation to the jury, not all outsiders are necessarily good people. Bob Ewell is an example. But the children learn that some outsiders they encounter (like Mayella Ewell) deserve their pity, and that others (like Mrs. Dubose) may be more complex than they at first discern. However, as Atticus also says, they all are human beings. They are also, in some way, victims.

Another element of this same theme, an element that incorporates numerous other characters, is the sympathetic bond that the children begin to acknowledge between themselves and the people who are so different from them. Part of the process of Scout's learning to know Boo Radley and the black people in Maycomb is Scout's coming to feel just how much of an outsider she is herself. As an avid reader, she is a freak in her first-grade class. As a tomboy, she is without little girl friends. As an independent-minded daughter of Atticus Finch, she is the object of brutal ridicule in the genteel ladies' missionary society.

A second theme that runs throughout the novel is that the laws and codes the town of Maycomb professes and lives by are always complex and often contradictory. The idea of law is raised at the start of the novel in the epigraph from Charles Lamb: "Lawyers, I suppose, were children once." The main adult character is a lawyer, and his two children seem destined to be lawyers. They are already at an early age familiar with legal terms. Their African-American housekeeper knows that things are different in the household of a lawyer, and she herself has learned to read from a classic book of law. Part One of the book, which develops the children's initiation into a world much uglier than the one they knew within the protective boundaries of their father's house, is built on legalities and social codes, both law-abiding and lawbreaking: Scout's "crime" of entering the first grade already knowing how to read, the long-ago arrest of Boo Radley and his friends for their loud behavior in the public square and Boo's second arrest for stabbing his father in the leg, the threat of lynching Tom Robinson, the charge of rape against him, the "entailments" of Mr. Cunningham, the illegal trespassing of the children on the Radley property, and the breaking of the hunting and truancy laws by the Ewells.

Most of Part Two is concerned with a trial and takes place in a courtroom. Here, most conversation is about legal matters concerning the constitution of juries and the penalty of death for rape. Finally, at the end of the story, Atticus and the sheriff break the law to protect Boo Radley from jail and from the community's attention after he has saved the children's lives by killing Bob Ewell.

A complication of this second theme is that even though the law should protect from evil and injustice the "mockingbirds" like Tom Robinson and Boo Radley and all those people of difference who are often victims of a homogeneous society, it has finally not been able to do so, mainly because hidden social codes contradict their stated legal and religious principles. For whatever reason, the law has been inadequate to protect Tom who is sent to prison and gets shot. It has also been inadequate to protect Boo, who is imprisoned by his father after a minor youthful skirmish with the law. And it is not the law that protects the children from Bob Ewell. Ironically, although the novel leads us to deplore the violence of the lynch mob that disrupts law, it is only an act of violence rather than law that protects the children from a literal mad dog and a human mad dog, Bob Ewell.

In summary, the two parts of the novel, which focus on the stories of two "mockingbirds" who are considered outlaws, are brought together through the various elements of the fiction to merge in a central theme of growing up to acknowledge the human bonds between ourselves and those so different from us.

Elements of Fiction

The novel is also successful because the multiple elements that make up the fiction support its themes. These elements consist of (1) point of view (or voice) and language, (2) tone, (3) time and place of setting, (4) characters, (5) plot structure, and (6) images and symbols.

In terms of the first element, it is clear that the author has developed a complex, first-person *point of view*. At the beginning and end of the novel, framing the story, is the point of view of the grown-up Scout (Jean Louise) looking back on the events of her childhood. Very quickly, however, another dimension is introduced, as we realize that the mature Scout is not simply recalling and interpreting the past but recalling it *as she had seen it as a child*. Much of the dialogue and narrative, for example, preserves the very young Scout's speech: it is told with the simple vocabulary and simple sentences of a young child, often fusing ungrammatical language and children's slang that we can't imagine the adult Scout using. For example, she says, "Miss Caroline was no more than twenty-one. She had bright auburn hair, pink cheeks, and wore crimson fingernail polish. She also wore high-heeled pumps and a red-and-white striped dress. She looked and smelled like a peppermint." There are, then, two levels of perception: the innocent view of the child, and the memory of the more knowing adult.

The *language* also combines (1) the rough dialogue of the boisterous children playing and fighting, with (2) the simple eloquence of Atticus's summation to the jury. Despite the characters' love of the written word, the novel seems to come out of a spoken rather than a written tradition. Just flipping through the pages reveals how much of it is conversation; for example, rather than having the adult narrator describe or explain a matter, we find that Atticus explains it in conversation with his brother or the children.

The second element of the novel's structure, closely related to voice, is tone. The tone of any work can range from flippant to ponderous. The *tone* of this novel, in keeping with the child's point of view, is simple rather than grandly eloquent. It is honest and direct rather than suggestive and secretive. As action involves the children's antics and perceptions, the tone is often comic. Descriptions of Scout's first day of school and her first snowman (or woman?) are good examples. At times, however, with simple, direct, and unemotional language, the tone soars into lofty, emotionally moving profundity—as when the Reverend Sykes instructs Scout to join the black people in the balcony in standing up in homage to her father. The lines are simple: "Miss Jean Louise, stand up. Your father's passin'." But the moment it creates is a highly charged one. The same is true of Atticus's discovery that the African-American community has brought a kitchenful of food to his house in appreciation of his efforts to help Tom Robinson, and of the moment when Scout turns to see Boo Radley in Jem's room and later as she looks down her street from the Radley porch and realizes that Boo has been looking out for them.

One of the most important elements in this fiction is the third one: *the time and place of its setting*. The setting of *To Kill a Mockingbird* is so vivid and exact that it seems at times to be a separate character. The time is the 1930s, when, the reader is told, massive unemployment and poverty plague the country. Franklin Roosevelt has just become President of the United States and, we are told, has given the nation some hope that the economic depression will be over. Part of the community has begun to take advantage of programs created by Roosevelt for economic relief. Everyone seems to be poor. Many have lost or are losing their land. Professional people like lawyers and doctors are paid in services and produce rather than cash. It is also a time, the novel reveals, when Adolf Hitler is rising to power in Europe, and it is already generally known that the persecution of Jews in Germany has begun.

This is the time of the setting. The place is the South, specifically southern Alabama—distinct not only from the northern United States but even from northern Alabama, which has industry, the state university, and a geographic/political element that did not secede from the Union during the Civil War. The South in this novel has been strongly influenced by the antebellum, cotton-growing plantation system and by defeat in the Civil War. The continuing influence of the plantation system and the war reveal themselves most decidedly in the attitudes toward race, the glorification of the past, the community's suspicion of outsiders, the lingering paternalism of some members of the more privileged class, and its tradition (on the surface) of polite and gentle manners. The South's defeat in the Civil War has contributed to the economic standstill of growth in the community and its removal from the rest of the world.

Typical attitudes toward race are especially evident in the town's reaction to Atticus's defense of Tom Robinson and in the views of the missionary society. Glorification of the past can be seen in Aunt Alexandra's somewhat ridiculous pride in her ancestors, even a relative who took a shot at the president of the University of Alabama. Suspicion of outsiders extends not only to the U.S. President's wife, Eleanor Roosevelt, but to the new young teacher from northern Alabama. Class snobbery is seen in Aunt Alexandra's obsession with what she regards as "good" or "old" families and her refusal to approve of Scout's playing with lower-class children. The tradition of paternalism, which seems a throwback to plantation days, is apparent in Atticus's assistance not only to Tom Robinson but also to Walter Cunningham, the dirt-poor farmer. Finally, typical southern courtliness is seen in the polite use of "Ma'am" and "Sir," in Atticus's gracious demeanor toward Mrs. Dubose, and in the attitude of respect adopted by children in the presence of adults.

Within the general setting of a small southern town are several arenas in which the action occurs: the house and yard of the Finch family, the elementary schoolhouse, the grounds around the Radley house, the Dubose house, Miss Maudie's yard, the street onto which these houses front, an African-American church, a courthouse, the street in front of the county jail, the house and yard of the Ewell family, and the yard in front of the Robinson family house. These arenas encompass particular institutions within the community: the family, the neighborhood, the public educational institution, the justice system, and the religious institution. Yet most are in some essential way corrupted or weakened and removed from the institutional ideal.

The fourth consideration is the *characters*, all of whom are Southerners. The major characters include the Finch family (the father Atticus, his daughter Scout, his son Jem, and his African-American housekeeper Calpurnia). Beyond the immediate Finch family, an equally important character is Dill, the young friend of the Finch children who spends his summers with relatives in Maycomb. These are the most important acting characters. In the next level of importance are the two characters who are chiefly acted upon: Tom Robinson, an African-American man accused of rape, and Boo Radley, whose presence is felt more in the children's minds than in actuality. Next are members of the extended Finch family and neighbors: Miss Maudie, a sympathetic, older friend of the children; the terrifying Mrs. Dubose; the ne'er-do-well Bob Ewell and his daughter Mayella; and Atticus's sister, the children's Aunt Alexandra.

The characters are at times divided into opposing camps, according to age or race or social status. At times, for example, the children seem to be opposed to the adults, the African-American characters at odds with the white characters, and the lower-class Old Sarum characters set apart from the townspeople.

At the same time, boundaries between these categories are often broken down momentarily, as when the children feel a kinship with the once-feared adult, Boo Radley, and when the adult Dolphus Raymond sympathizes with the children's disgust at the trial. Barriers between classes are broken down when an Old Sarum child is a luncheon guest in the Finch household; and lines between the races are broken down when the children attend a black church, when they later sit with the black spectators in the courthouse balcony, and when Scout asks to visit Calpurnia's house.

The common denominator in all the white characters is their southernness and their eccentricity. The classic eccentric is Boo Radley, who has
been locked up by his father for most of his life and who, gossip has it, lurks
about at night feeding on raw animals. But actually each one of the major
white characters can be described as "peculiar" in some essential way. Scout
Finch is a precocious little girl who dresses in overalls, curses, and beats up
little boys. Her brother, Jem, is a loner who, like Scout, calls his father by his
first name. Atticus, their father, is also an eccentric in that he does not hunt
or fish or participate in sports, as other men in this community do. Dill, the
children's friend, is a child sent away by his mother to live much of the year
with distant relatives. He lives largely in an imagined world, spinning
fantastic tales about being kidnapped, for example, which he relates to his
two friends. All the neighbors who live on the street are eccentric. Miss
Maudie hates her house, spends most of her time gardening with overalls on,
amuses the children by sticking out her false teeth, and is not above shouting
rejoinders to some churchgoers who claim she loves flowers too much. Mrs.
Dubose is a drug addict who screams insults at the children when they pass
her house. Dolphus Raymond, who lives in the country, pretends to be drunk
all the time to give the community a reason for his decision to live with an
African-American wife and children. Bob Ewell lives on welfare, whatever he
scavenges from the garbage dump near his house, and the game he kills out
of season.

Plot structure is the fifth element of fiction that embodies the major
ideas of the novel. The novel is framed by the comments of the adult
narrator, but the story within that frame is chronologically developed; it
covers a period of two and a half years, from the time Scout is six until the
fall of her eighth year. The action is divided into two main parts. The first
primarily develops the children's approach to Boo Radley, their unseen
neighbor. The second part is the story of the trial of Tom Robinson for rape.
Each part consists of distinct episodes.

Part One offers the following episodes:

1. Scout, Jem, and Dill spend their first summer together, when
   they begin approaching Boo Radley.

2. Scout is able to endure her first year at school when Boo
   Radley contacts the children through the hole in the tree.

3. During the second summer Scout rolls in a tire against the
   Radley house, the children begin the Radley drama, and Jem
   tries to see in the Radleys' windows at night.

4. In the fall of the next school year, Mr. Radley plasters up the hole in the tree, it snows, and Boo puts a blanket around Scout's shoulder during the fire.

5. During Christmas of that year, Scout beats up her cousin Francis and the Robinson theme is introduced.

6. In February Atticus shoots a mad dog.

7. In the spring Jem is forced to read to Mrs. Dubose.

Part Two has fewer distinct episodes:

1. The children visit Calpurnia's church.

2. Aunt Alexandra's arrival causes conflict.

3. During the next summer Atticus faces a lynch mob.

4. Tom Robinson is tried for rape.

5. Scout has to face the missionary society and the death of Tom Robinson.

6. The children are attacked on the way home from a Halloween party in the fall.

The action of the novel is unified by the fact that it opens and closes with Boo Radley. Furthermore, the Tom Robinson and Boo Radley sections are integrally connected, in that two characters and what they represent are united in their identification with the mockingbird of the title. Like the mockingbird, they are vulnerable and harmless creatures who are at the mercy of an often unreasonable and cruel society.

The mockingbird brings us to the sixth consideration in a discussion of the elements of fiction: the novel's *imagery and symbolism*, the central figure of which is the mockingbird. Atticus and Miss Maudie explain that to kill a mockingbird is a sin because it is a harmless creature that gives others its song. Tom Robinson and Boo Radley are clearly identified with the mockingbird: Mr. Underwood, the Maycomb newspaper editor, "likened Tom's death to the senseless slaughter of songbirds by hunters and children"; and when Atticus and Sheriff Tate contemplate the effect of arresting Boo Radley for murder, Scout interjects, "Well, it'd be sort of like shootin' a mocking-bird, wouldn't it?"

Other, less prominent symbols are interwoven in the text. Mrs. Dubose's camellias, for example, appear to be images of an old southern frame of mind that defies defeat. Although the flowers are beautiful, they are clearly associated with the insane racism and cruelty spewed out by Mrs. Dubose, an aged southern aristocrat who supposedly keeps a Confederate gun close at hand. When Jem destroys her camellias, he is lashing out at the attitudes she represents.

The columns or pillars, looking somewhat out of place on the court-house, also exemplify an outmoded, antebellum, plantation way of life and attitudes that continue to surface.

The rabid dog that Atticus shoots is a symbolic foreboding of his attempt to save the community from committing an act of madness. And guns themselves in the novel represent a kind of violence and savagery, an abuse of power, that Atticus has tried to avoid even though he is a sharp-shooter. Miss Maudie believes that Atticus decided to lay down his gun when he realized it gave him an unfair advantage over dumb animals.

Each element of the fiction—point of view, tone, setting, characteriza-tion, plot structure, and imagery—plays an integral part in the advancement of the novel's major themes.

COLIN NICHOLSON

Hollywood and Race: To Kill a Mockingbird

Nothing, it would seem, could be much faster than the ability of the reader's eye to move across the printed page, processing linguistic information, absorbing it and 'staging' it in the imagination. Almost instantaneously, the mind decodes the words on the page, translating complex messages into images, into imagined events. On the cinema screen, however, things move even faster. The viewer encounters several sign systems at once. These include spoken language, musical accompaniment and pictorial event and the viewer is bombarded with additional modes of communication. Novel readers thus exercise much greater control over their responses, and over the time taken to digest and respond to them, than do film spectators.

In the case of the literary and filmic texts of *To Kill a Mockingbird*, these differences of pace and control are in some ways intensified. Harper Lee's celebrated novel of the American South is leisurely, reasoned and reflective. As directed by Robert Mulligan, the film of the book moves with considerable speed, selecting and compressing incidents into a relatively short running time, so that several themes developed in the narrative space of the novel are necessarily compressed in the film's option to concentrate upon the central theme of racial hostility towards blacks by Southern whites. In the novel there are repeated image-patterns and themes which provide a context and a sense of depth for this central concern of racial prejudice. The care

From *Cinema and Fiction: New Modes of Adapting, 1950-1990.* © 1992 by Edinburgh University Press.

89

with which a family history is integrated into a wider sense of the history of the Southern States: the theme of family relationships, of journeying both literal and metaphorical out of childhood, of religious hypocrisy; all these, if they survive in the film, survive only at fleeting moments, and not as fundamental parts of the fabric of the story as they indubitably are in Lee's novel.

The novel is narrated by Jean Louise Finch, one of the central characters, from the perspective of an adult remembering events from her own childhood. As a child she was known as 'Scout', and because she had lived through these experiences *before* she begins to record them as an adult in written form, Scout reports for us more than she properly realises she is seeing. It is a familiar literary technique in first-person narration, and here, in the tension between what Scout saw as a child and what she understands as a remembering adult, we are able to follow the steps of her development from innocence to maturity. Since the focus of the novel is on Scout's brother, Jem, he becomes the main character, with the reader observing Scout's changing awareness through the characterisation of Jem and through her own relationship to him. In such ways, the Finch children, together with Dill, remain the centre of attention throughout the book.

The obvious and frequent corollary in American film of a remembering first-person narrator in fiction is the use of the 'voice-over' technique. When Scout first comes into view on screen, her adult voice is already speaking words on the sound-track which closely approximate to those used in the novel. But the star system of the Hollywood studio productions of the sixties changed the focus of the novel in crucial ways. In the screen version, Scout's father, Atticus Finch (Gregory Peck), becomes the central character. The American white male, cast here in the heroic figure of a progressive liberal lawyer fighting for the civil rights of a black man falsely accused of raping a young white woman, dominates the action. This shifts our attention onto the campaigning for, and survival of, the rights and principles of racial justice which are denied to the accused African-American, Tom Robinson. The film's concentration on the father, stressed throughout by the camera's constant attention to Peck, is seen particularly in the sequence where Atticus shoots the mad dog. The camera lingers on Jem's open-mouthed admiration for his father's mastery with guns. Atticus may be an American liberal, but even though his spectacles slip symbolically from his eyes as he aims the gun, he shares, in both film and book, the masculine prowess which a wider American culture considers to be important. As the all-powerful father-figure, Atticus displaces the children as the source of developing awareness. Hence his dominance and authority on the screen narrow the film's scope and range.

The deeply ironic schoolroom discussion of American democracy and German fascism, which takes place in Chapter 26 of the novel, is only the most obvious case in point. The smug complacency of Miss Gates does much to prepare the Finch children and the reader for the gap between Maycomb's opinion of itself as a town, and the stark actuality revealed by things which are to come. It contributes a considerable amount towards the experience and understanding of Jem and Scout, and provides a cutting counterpoint to their forthcoming live encounter with racism and persecution in the small Southern town. But all of this is omitted from the picture, as is the novel's extensive satire on religious hypocrisy. Another crucial omission is the novel's repeated reference to and detailed treatment of family structure and family life. From Dill's status as unwanted child to the repression in the Radley household and the Ewell poverty and violence, the greater narrative attention of the novel enables it to explore the often painful experience of family influences. In this respect the Finch family household proves the most interesting, with the black servant Calpurnia becoming accepted as a surrogate mother-figure, though there is no verbal reference in the film to the fact of her colour, and the children form relationships which cross over the immediate ties of blood-kinship.

In the film the viewer sees things immediately, through a camera which is always allied to Scout, the narrator's, perception. As a result there is an inevitable slackening of the narrative tension which generates some of the novel's most powerful effects. Conversely the immediacy of film enables Mulligan's picture to register the shock impact of unsettling experiences on the children. The novel, however, remains more powerful. Consideration of the image of the mockingbird might help us to understand the process whereby some things are lost in the transition to film mode. In the opening lines we read:

> When he was nearly thirteen, my brother Jem got his arm badly broken at the elbow. When it healed, and Jem's fears of never being able to play football were assuaged, he was seldom self-conscious about his injury. His left arm was somewhat shorter than his right; when he stood or walked, the back of his hand was at right-angles to his body, his thumb parallel to his thigh. He couldn't have cared less so long as he could pass and punt.

The careful attention to detail here suggests that this is a self-conscious piece of narrative foreshadowing, looking forward as it does to the vicious attack upon the Finch children by Bob Ewell, an attack which does not take place until the novel's penultimate chapter. Such things cast a shadow forward, as well as registering that this is, in fact, a discourse of memory, a personal history the outcome of which is known to the narrator, though not to the reader. But it is rather more than that, too.

Whereas in the film there is virtually only one mockingbird, that is to say only one victim, the accused Tom Robinson; in the novel several characters besides Jem Finch are at one time or another considered in that light. Much play is made, in the film's climactic court-room scene, with the fact that Tom Robinson's left arm hung dead at his side, the result of an accident with a cotton-gin which meant that it was anyway impossible for him to have raped anyone in the way his supposed victim had described it. The novelistic foreshadowing, which suggests that Jem Finch is also in some sense a mockingbird and that his experiences of racism have damaged him and, in his transition from childhood to adulthood, left him permanently scarred, is passed over in the film. Images which give the novel a kind of depth and range, are omitted leaving Atticus's court-room remark to echo reductively in the film version: 'This case is as simple as black and white.'

Nor can this be attributed solely to the inevitable selection and compression which must take place in the translation of a novel into film, since this film demonstrates an ability to find correlatives for the novel's backward-looking narrative structure. Quite apart from the voice-over technique of Jean-Louise's adult voice, the film makes suggestive and subtle uses of childhood images in its opening sequence as the credits roll and before the film narrative proper begins. As a visual equivalent to the novel's adult narrator re-creating the world of her own childhood beginnings, we watch a child's hands shaping the letters of the film's title—a kind of writing—and we see a child's hands drawing an image of a mockingbird. While this image is being made, the camera pans across a watch, symbol of time passing, and itself an image which recurs in the film. Then, the child drawing the bird tears the paper, 'killing' the mockingbird and leaving a jagged image of white on black; the camera continues to pan across, the different toys and objects left by Boo Radley for the children to collect from the tree-knot outside the Radley house. Spilled from the toy-box which normally contains all of these items, we see a penknife, which foreshadows two subsequent events in Boo Radley's life: the attack upon his father, and much more significantly, his slaying of Bob Ewell at the time of the latter's attack upon Scout and Jem. We also see two carved figures, perhaps representing the two Finch children.

That toy-box forms a part of the film's own reference back upon itself in much the same way that the novel's narrative is a return to time past. On the evening of the day when Nathan Radley cements up the knot-hole in the tree, Jem shows Scout all of the objects which have been left for them by Boo. 'It was to be a long time before Jem and I talked about Boo again,' says the adult voice-over. Then a hand closes the toy-box which takes us back to the film's opening sequence. Such use of images suggests several possible ways in which film can find its own equivalents and correlatives for techniques of continuity, recall and foreshadowing used in narrative fiction.

Perhaps one of the most striking of these connects the small-town atmosphere of Maycomb ('a tired old town'), static and enclosed, with a particular tendency in the film's camera-work. On page 11 of the novel we read words which are remarkably close to the opening sentences of the film's screenplay: 'A day was twenty-four hours long but seemed longer. There was no hurry, for there was nowhere to go; nothing to buy and no money to buy it with'. This is taken almost word-perfect into the screenplay. The end of the novel's sentence—'nothing to see outside the boundaries of Maycomb County'—is omitted, perhaps because Hollywood sought a wider American audience for the film's narrowing of focus onto the theme of racial prejudice. But that oppressive, self-regarding community is explored in a variety of ways in the novel's leisurely space. Given the more intense demands of unity in film-time, such space is not available.

From the opening camera-shot, a shift from looking upwards to trees and outwards to the sky beyond, down onto the practically deserted streets of Maycomb, we gradually become aware that the severely restricted camera-movement throughout the film is having particular effects. When the children peer over the fence into the Radley house, the camera slides conspiratorially up behind them: as they move around the side of the house, the camera arcs upwards, to look down on them. In the courtroom scene the camera moves into close-up on Tom Robinson's face as he gives his evidence. Clever editing during the moment of Ewell's assault upon the children gives the impression of rapidity and confusion. And for the final shot, in a sense reversing the open movement down onto the streets of Maycomb, the camera tracks away from Jem's bedroom, and away from the Finch household. With the exception of these shaping movements, the camera is remarkably static during the film narrative; sometimes tracking slightly to the left or right, but more predominantly remaining fixed, unmoving. Even when Atticus drives from Maycomb proper to where Tom Robinson's wife Helen and the rest of the segregated Negro community live, we see only the car's departure and arrival. In all these ways, any sense of movement is kept to minimal levels, and the overall atmosphere of stasis and enclosure reinforced.

Both novel and film suffer from being sentimentalised narratives. One reviewer of the film commented:

> Harper Lee's *To Kill a Mockingbird* is one of the best recent examples of the sentimental novel: the book designed principally to

create warmth, which doesn't exclude ugliness but views it through generally optimistic eyes . . . is not vigorous enough to celebrate life, but does enjoy it.

The scene early in the film, where Jem and Scout discuss their dead mother while the camera lingers on Gregory Peck's listening expression out on the front-porch is a case in point. Or, perhaps to more obviously engineered effect, when, at the conclusion of the court scene, Scout tells us, 'I looked around. They were standing. All around us and in the balcony on the opposite wall, the Negroes were getting to their feet.' With Reverend Sykes's comment, film and novel indulge in the creation of sentimental emotion towards the idealising of Atticus Finch: 'Miss Jean Louise, stand up. Your Father's passin'.'

Moreover, both versions veer at other times—and frequently—towards the melodramatic, and on at least one occasion the film seems better able to keep a sense of greater realism, even at a moment of high melodrama. In the novel, during the scene when Jem, Scout and Dill arrive at the jailhouse where a lynch-mob has gathered, the staginess of the affair is accentuated: 'I sought once more for a familiar face, and at the centre of the semi-circle, I found one.' It is Mr Cunningham, and Scout proceeds to address him on the matter of his entailment and concerning their family relationships in the closed community of Maycomb, reminding Mr Cunningham to say 'hey' to his son Walter on Scout's behalf. The unreality of the scene is further conveyed:

> when I slowly awoke to the fact that I was addressing the entire aggregation. The men were all looking at me, some had their mouths half open. Atticus had stopped poking Jem: they were standing together beside Dill. Their attention amounted to fascination.

In the silence which follows Scout's speech, the novel records that she:

> looked around and up at Mr Cunningham, whose face was equally impassive. Then he did a peculiar thing. He squatted down and took me by both shoulders. 'I'll tell him you said hey, little lady,' he said before leading the mob away.

Both film and novel wish to stress the creative goodness of childhood, even in such extremes of situation. Perhaps realising that when translated into visual terms such a transformation of Cunningham from angry potential lyncher into softened and caring father might stretch the bounds of credibility, the film opts for registering the acute embarrassment of Cunningham's sideways glance—he is obviously too disconcerted to face Scout directly while she is talking—before he mutters the response included in both versions. Within the margins of a highly melodramatic and unlikely resolution of the scene, the film is slightly more satisfying than the novel.

When, however, melodrama passes over into a more gothic mode, when aspects of mystery and of terror at the unknown form part of the narrative—the film often seems better able to convey a sense of threat, of suspense and of shadowy uncertainty. For the children involved, the figure of Boo Radley is one such gothic dimension, a character who in many ways typifies an identifiable strand in American fiction from the Southern States. Again, for the children, the Radley household figures as the equivalent of a gothic mansion:

> Inside the house lived a malevolent phantom. People said he existed, but Jem and I had never seen him. People said he went out at night when the moon was high, and peeped in windows . . .
> A Negro would not pass the Radley place at night, he would cut across to the sidewalk opposite and whistle as he walked.

Although this provides Harper Lee with ample opportunity for comic insight into the workings of childhood imagination and superstition, we also realise that the bogey figure of Boo Radley serves as a symbolic figure of more serious dimensions. Not only is he both sign and representative of an oppressive and inhibited society which, rather than face up to them, is far happier suppressing home truths that are shaming, he is also by that same token a mark of embarrassment to his own family as well as a signal of the repressive intolerance in a wider community.

Aided by Elmer Bernstein's musical score, the film's judicious use of light and shadow, and in particular its presentation of night sequences as the children pursue Dill's idea of 'making Boo Radley come out,' catches this mood and feeling of the uncanny and the mysterious. When Jem stays at home on guard, while Atticus takes the black servant Calpurnia home (Calpurnia, of course, sitting on the back seat of the car), Jem sits in the swing chair on the front porch, hearing a screech-owl as shadows of leaves cast black and white patterns on his face. Frightened, he runs down the street after his father's car, shouting 'Atticus.' Outside the Radley house he hears their swing-chair creaking in the wind, and knocking against the woodwork. At this moment he finds the first of the objects left in the tree-knot by Boo. Hearing the sound of the screech-owl again, he takes to his heels and heads for home. The camera repeatedly plays upon that creaking swing-chair on the Radley porch, but even so, this whole aspect of the story is expertly condensed into that cinematic moment when in order to 'get a look at Boo Radley,' Jem, watched fearfully by Scout and Dill, crawls one evening onto the Radley porch. As he peeps through the window, he is approached by a figure casting a looming, threatening shadow which is seen first by the viewer watching the film, then by Scout and Dill, then again by the viewer. When a shadowy hand reaches out to touch Jem, all three children crouch in terror; the figure, starkly stage-lit to register black upon white, withdraws and the three children run for their lives. Symbolic overtone, as well as melodramatic event are registered together. And towards the film's close, Boo Radley, at Scout's invitation, does touch the unconscious Jem's forehead, bringing to the surface, and out into the open a relationship that had hitherto remained unclear and incomplete.

Boo Radley ends by helping the children at a decisive moment, and anyway makes them presents during the progress of the story, those presents with which the film opens. But the way in which Boo saves the children, and more importantly the reaction of the authorities to his intervention, brings us into an area where both texts appear to be complicit in the very values they seek to reform. Much more so than in the novel, the film makes great play with the court scene, devoting to it a disproportionate amount of playing time. It is the scene in which the central values of democratic justice and common decency come into conflict with racial prejudice so deeply rooted that it overturns utterly convincing evidence of Tom Robinson's innocence. But although there may be dramatic reasons for Atticus Finch's defence and celebration of America's legal procedures—after all, he is concerned primarily to sway the opinions of a jury whose biases he knows only too well—none the less the words he uses stand in sharp opposition to the actual practices of the court and its jurors.

In the major summing-up speech for the defence, some passages from the novel are altered in their sequence, but with minor exceptions the language is the same. Atticus Finch, played with style and conviction by Gregory Peck, asserts that 'there is one institution in which all men are created equal,' and he continues, 'in this country our courts are the great levellers.' Then, of the integrity of the jury system, he claims 'that is no ideal to me, it is a living working reality. Gentlemen, a court is no better than any man of you sitting before me on this jury. A court is only as sound as its jury, and a jury is only as sound as the men who make it up.' The first irony which strikes us is the obvious one that no women could serve on juries in Alabama at that time. To have black men serve was unthinkable. But the film makes a telling point in this respect. Although the three children, symbols of warmth, light and innocence, sit next to Reverend Sykes, the court is otherwise rigidly segregated. This is dramatically focused for us when the pronouncement is made: 'will the defendant please rise and face the jury.' What happens is that the camera does not turn to the jury, but to the people who are in fact Tom Robinson's peers and equals—the black community sitting up in the court-room gallery. It is a brief shot, but it carries considerable cinematic weight in terms of its irony and social comment.

Given the horrors that overtake Tom Robinson after a guilty verdict is returned, the whole of the court scene creates serious problems for the readers' and viewers' attitudes towards the sentimental warmth with which much of the story unfolds. Overall, both novel and film serve to vindicate the liberal values of domestic and civic virtue which the Finch household represents. The reviewer for *Newsweek* makes the appropriate comment on this problem:

> In a seemingly leisurely way, the novel drifted through 121 pages of youthful adventure, and, only then, with the children solidly established did it turn into a rape case. The two discrete parts of the novel are telescoped in the film, however, and the result is to bring the trial out of the blurry background and into sharp focus. The trial weighed upon the novel, and in the film, where it is heavier, it is unsupportable. The narrator's voice returns at the end, full of warmth and love . . . but we do not pay her the same kind of attention any more. We have seen that outrageous trial, and we can no longer share the warmth of her love.

That sentimental warmth helps to create the conditions for a tidily 'happy' ending, an ending that further suggests that problems have been raised which the authoress, and following her the director Robert Mulligan, cannot finally resolve. Brendon Gill writing in *The New Yorker* makes the point:

> In the last few minutes of the picture, whatever intellectual and moral content it may be said to have contained is crudely tossed away in order to provide a 'happy' ending. Peck . . . and the sheriff agree to pretend that a wicked white man who has been killed will be reported to have fallen on his own knife, thus sparing the man who killed him—admittedly a mental case, but the saviour of the lawyer's children—the humiliation of a public arraignment. The moral of this can only be that while ignorant rednecks mustn't take the law into their own hands, it's all right for *nice* people to do so.

If Boo Radley has cast a shadow upon the development of the children throughout the unfolding story, the way in which his killing of Bob Ewell is covered up by those in authority leaves the unavoidable impression that for Maycomb, and by extension for Alabama more generally, 'Law' and its 'Order' are to be manipulated by those who, it is presumed, know best. *To Kill a Mockingbird* generates serious moral and social issues. But in order to bring them to a satisfying conclusion, film and book take refuge in the very suppression of truth and deception of a community which the assumed story has attempted to expose.

CAROLYN JONES

Atticus Finch and the Mad Dog:
Harper Lee's To Kill a Mockingbird

One must think like a hero to behave
like a merely decent human being.
—May Sarton

In the Spring of 1960, in the midst of the major events of the civil rights movement, J. B. Lippincott and Company published Harper Lee's *To Kill A Mockingbird*. A Pulitzer Prize winner which was made later into an Academy Award-winning film, the novel became and remains a bestseller. Yet, this novel which captured the imagination while it criticized the morality of American adults is classified as "young adult literature." This classification has caused the work to be ignored by the critical community and has undercut the power of the image of the modern hero that it presents. The dominant voice of *To Kill A Mockingbird* is not that of a child but that of a woman looking back at an event that tore at the fabric of childhood and of her community and that shaped her adulthood.

To Kill A Mockingbird is about three years (approximately 1933–1936) in the childhood of Jean Louise Finch, better known as Scout, and the coming of age of Scout and her brother Jem in the household of their father, Atticus Finch. It is also about two seemingly unrelated things—the

From *The Southern Quarterly* 34:4 (Summer 1996). © 1996 by the University of Southern Mississippi.

trial of a black man, Tom Robinson, for rape and the attempts of Jem, Scout and their friend Dill to make Boo Radley come out of his house. Boo, a man who, for his lifetime, is confined to his house, first, by his father and, later, by his uncle for committing a minor offense as a teenager, becomes a catalyst for the imagination and a symbol by which the children come to understand, in their particular ways, Tom Robinson's trial. For Jem, the boy coming into manhood, the desire to see Boo is abandoned with Tom's conviction, and Jem moves into the adult world. For Scout, however, who is a child of about nine, Boo becomes the source of her imagination and the inspiration for her career as a writer. Thus, *To Kill A Mockingbird* shows the reader the importance of the imagination in the formation of the moral human being.

Yet, the children do not reach their understandings of Boo and Tom alone. The relationship of Boo Radley to Tom Robinson is mediated by Atticus Finch, the hero of the novel. Through the actions and thoughts of her father, Scout is able to make sense of Boo and Tom as she criticizes the morality of 1930s and 1960s America. Atticus's moral structure gives form to the imagination that Scout's meeting with Boo fires. Atticus is not the typical modern hero: he is neither angst-ridden nor decontextualized. He is a widower, a father, a lawyer and a neighbor—in short, an ordinary man living his life in a community. Yet, he stands as a supreme example of the moral life, and he communicates that morality to his children and, ultimately, to the community by his actions. Atticus's ordinary heroism embodies three components: the call for critical reflection on the self, the rule of compassion, and the law that it is a sin to kill a mockingbird. This heroism is illustrated in three key scenes in which he confronts mad dogs.

The first of these scenes introduces the theme of the mad dog and its importance to the novel. Jem and Scout have been bemoaning the fact that their father is the most uninteresting man in town; "Our father," Scout tells us, "didn't do anything." When he gives Jem and Scout air rifles for Christmas, he also refuses to teach them to shoot. This winter, however, is one of amazing portents, foreshadowing the trial of Tom Robinson and the emergence of Boo Radley: it snows for the first time in years; the Finchs' neighbor, Miss Maudie's house burns down; and a mad dog named Tim Johnson appears in February on the main street of Maycomb.

Heck Tate, the sheriff, refuses to shoot the mad dog himself. Much to the children's amazement—they nearly fainted, Scout says—Tate turns the job over to Atticus.

> In a fog, Jem and I watched our father take the gun and walk out
> into the middle of the street. He walked quickly, but I thought he

moved like an underwater swimmer: time had slowed to a nause-
ating crawl.

Atticus pushed his glasses to his forehead; they slipped down,
and he dropped them in the street. In the silence, I heard them
crack. Atticus rubbed his eyes and chin; we saw him blink hard.

In front of the Radley gate, Tim Johnson had made up what
was left of his mind. He had finally turned himself around, to
pursue his original course up our street. He made two steps
forward, then stopped and raised his head. We saw his body go
rigid.

With movements so swift they seemed simultaneous, Atticus'
hand yanked a ball-tipped lever as he brought the gun to his
shoulder.

The rifle cracked. Tim Johnson leaped, flopped over and
crumpled on the sidewalk in a brown-and-white heap. He didn't
know what hit him.

What Tim Johnson sees when he raises his head is Atticus Finch. Atticus
allows himself to be the target of an irrational force and to absorb its violence
as he acts to protect innocent people. This stance, his putting himself
between the innocent and danger, characterizes the man. And this action,
which occurs two more times in the novel, thematically binds the
rite-of-passage of Jem and Scout to the rape trial of Tom Robinson and to
the emergence of Boo Radley.

Mad dogs are easy; the courage to deal with a mad dog involves taking
a concrete action: picking up a gun and shooting. Human beings are difficult;
to respect their humanity, especially when they are wrong, makes concrete
action difficult. In defending Tom Robinson, Atticus has to find a way both
to respect the humanity of even his most belligerent opponents and to
protect his innocent client. The alleged rape of Mayella Ewell presents the
white citizens of Maycomb with something that "makes men lose their heads
[so that] they couldn't be fair if they tried." Like the dog infected with rabies,
the citizens of Maycomb are infected with Maycomb's "usual disease,"
racism, which makes them just as irrational and just as dangerous as Tim
Johnson. Atticus's neighbors and friends, therefore, are those "mad dogs"
that he must confront. In an attempt to confront their irrational fears and to
educate them that "Maycomb had . . . nothing to fear but fear itself," Atticus
must find a different kind of courage than that of picking up a gun, the kind
of courage that one has when "you know you are licked before you begin but
you begin anyway and you see it through no matter what." This definition of
courage provides the transition from facing the animal in the street to facing

the citizens of Maycomb. Atticus, throughout the novel, then, repeats morally the stance that he takes physically in the city street.

That physical and moral stance embodies two philosophical components. The first is Atticus's "dangerous question," "Do you really think so?" and the second is Atticus's admonition to Scout to stand in another person's shoes before judging him or her. Fred Erisman, in "The Romantic Regionalism of Harper Lee," calls Atticus Finch an Emersonian hero who is able to cast a skeptical eye on the conventional ideas of goodness, to supplant those virtues that have lost their value, and to preserve those that work. Edwin Burrell, playing on Atticus's name, says Atticus is "no heroic type but [is like] any graceful, restrained, simple person like one from Attica." Burrell sees Atticus as the Greek rational hero: "Know thyself. Nothing too much." Both are correct, as far as they take their arguments. Both account for Atticus's self-knowledge, but neither attempts to bind the "Know thyself" to Atticus's equally powerful assertion that we must know others as well. How can these be reconciled?

To ask the question "Do you really think so?" asks us to begin to understand ourselves by articulating the meaning of the actions and thoughts that, often, are reflections of the unspoken values of our communities. Alasdair MacIntyre, in *After Virtue*, reminds us that we inherit such values along with our bonds of family, city, tribe and nation. These relationships "constitute the given of my life, my moral starting point." The moral inheritance of the whites of Maycomb includes set ways in which to see those different from themselves, particularly blacks. Their assumptions about blacks are, as Atticus says in his closing argument "that *all* Negroes lie, that *all* Negroes are basically immoral beings, that *all* Negro men are not to be trusted around our women." Atticus, through his defense of Tom Robinson and by his very presence, brings into question these assumptions, forcing those ideas to become conscious and, perhaps, to be articulated. His question invites expression but is also threatening because of its disorienting effect. "Do you really think so?" forces us to confront our deepest beliefs, dreams and fears.

James Baldwin gives us an example of this kind of confrontation in an essay on Martin Luther King, in which he recalled the silence that he encountered on an integrated bus not long after the Montgomery boycott was settled:

> This silence made me think of nothing so much as the silence which follows a really serious lovers' quarrel: the whites, beneath their cold hostility, were mystified and deeply hurt. They had been betrayed by the Negroes, not merely because the Negroes had declined to remain in their "place," but

because the Negroes had refused to be controlled by the town's image of them. And without this image, it seemed to me, the whites were abruptly and totally lost. The very foundations of their private and public worlds were being destroyed.

This angry silence indicates that the white people resist and resent the change in the structure and story that has guided and undergirded their lives. Atticus's question potentially breaks through the kind of silence that Baldwin encountered on that Montgomery bus, forcing that silence to speak, perhaps creating a dialogue, between the self and the "other." Atticus, the man, becomes the catalyst for this dialogue in Maycomb.

Maycomb is, Scout tells us, "an old town . . . an old tired town." It has been, as Erisman points out, "a part of southern Alabama from the time of the first settlements, and isolated and largely untouched by the Civil War, it was, like the South, turned inward upon itself by Reconstruction. Indeed its history parallels that of the South in so many ways that it emerges as a microcosm of the South." Maycomb clings to its ideals, its traditions and its rigid caste system as ways of affirming its identity. People, especially blacks and poor whites, are, as Baldwin noted, expected to remain in their "places." The alleged rape of Mayella Ewell violates this order and throws the town and the individuals involved into confrontation with their community identity.

Atticus, in the second mad dog incident, confronts two very different sets of Maycomb's white citizenry, both with the same assumptions. The first group is "good" citizens—"merchants, in-town farmers," even the town doctor—who come to warn Atticus that Tom Robinson is in danger. They ultimately confront Atticus about his defending a black man who has been accused of raping a white woman and tell Atticus that he has everything to lose. Atticus asks, "Do you really think so?" The men, angered, advance on Atticus: "There was a murmur among the group of men, made more ominous when Atticus moved back to the bottom front step and the men drew nearer to him." The tension is broken when Jem, afraid for his father, yells to Atticus that the phone is ringing.

Not long after, Scout disperses the second group of Maycomb's citizens—this time, poor white citizens who smell of stale whiskey and the pigpen—who come to the jail to lynch Tom Robinson. Scout watches her father push back his hat, fold his newspaper and confront the angry men. The men assume that Atticus is powerless because they have called away the sheriff, but Atticus's response is "Do you really think so?" Scout, hearing the question for the second time that evening, thinks this is "too good to miss" and runs to see what is going to happen. Scout's presence and her personalization of the mob, her singling out Mr. Cunningham, the father of one of her school friends, disrupts the mob psychology, ending the danger. Only later does Scout realize the implications of what she has witnessed:

> I was very tired, and was drifting into sleep when the memory of Atticus calmly folding his newspaper and pushing back his hat became Atticus standing in the middle of an empty waiting street, pushing up his glasses. The full meaning of the night's awful events hit me and I began crying.

Atticus's question penetrates to the heart of the images and ideas that sustain the citizens of Maycomb as surely as the bullet penetrates the body of the mad dog. Faced with a challenge to their identity, both groups of men react; they lose their reason and become like a mad dog, attacking the man who calls their truth into question.

Why do the children have to save Atticus? Herein lies another dimension of the problem and potential danger of Atticus's question. Atticus's Apollonian virtues are based on the assumption that he is dealing with rational and reflective people. Scout indicates that when Atticus asks the question of her and Jem, he follows the question with a lesson or proof that forces the two of them to prove the validity of their ideas:

> "Do you really think so?"
> This was Atticus's dangerous question. "Do you really think you want to move there, Scout?" Bam, bam, bam, and the checkerboard was swept clean of my men. "Do you really think that, son? Then read this." Jem would struggle the rest of an evening through the speeches of Henry W. Grady.

What reforming action can Atticus offer to these angry and emotional men confronted with a black man whom they think has gotten "above his place"? None. Tom Robinson is not part of their community in any vital and human way. They do not *see* Tom Robinson. He is not one of them; he exists either outside of the community or on its periphery. He is not their neighbor, either in the literal or in the religious sense. Atticus forces the men, if they cannot see Tom Robinson, to see Atticus Finch. Their anger, however, nearly makes them forget that they *do* consider Atticus their neighbor. Only the intervention of the children restores their reason. Reflection, however, can take the men only as far as the experience of Atticus Finch; to see Tom Robinson, another kind of action is demanded. The first half of Atticus's ethic, the demand for reflection, therefore, is useless without the second half, the standing in another's shoes, the demand for compassion.

Civilization can be seen as "the agreement, slowly arrived at, to let the abyss alone," as Alan Tate says in *The Fathers* (185–86). Then, the Tom Robinsons of the world are defined as the abyss around which we create impenetrable boundaries. Or civilization can be a structure based on compassion—on the fact that, as Martin Luther King, Jr. said in *Strength to Love*, the "other" "is a part of me and I am a part of him. His agony diminishes me, and his salvation enlarges me." Compassion has limits: it contains the realization that I can never know your experience as you experience it, but that I can, because of our "human fellow feeling," as Joseph Conrad termed it, make an attempt to know what you feel and, thereby, bring you into the narrative of my experience. Hermeneutics creates the neighbor.

Atticus explains this to Scout as walking in another person's shoes:

> "First of all," he said, "if you can learn a simple trick, Scout, you'll get along a lot better with all kinds of folks. You never really understand a person until you consider things from his point of view . . . until you climb into his skin and walk around in it."

Atticus asks Scout to "see with" others, to be compassionate. But compassion must be bound to the critical question "Do you really think so?" in order to respect the humanity of the neighbor. Critique without compassion threatens to become force; compassion without critique may dissolve into sentimentalism or emotionalism. Either stance alone turns the "I" into an "It," either an object to be controlled or a creature to be stereotyped or pitied. Both are required in order to see clearly, and though they may not lead to truth, they often lead, as Atticus tells Scout, to compromise. Reflection gives us humility, forces us to confront our own frailties and limitations; and compassion helps us love, lets us make, as Iris Murdoch says, "the connection of knowledge with love and of spiritual insight with apprehension of the unique." Scout will exercise this ethic in the most essential way at the end of the novel.

In the third of the mad dog scenes, the trial of Tom Robinson becomes a symbol for the attempt to stand in another's shoes and see an event from that person's perspective while maintaining a critical capacity. Attic says that serving on a jury "'forces a man to make up his mind and declare himself about something. Men don't like to do that.'" This case not only questions the jury, but it questions Atticus himself. When Scout learns that Atticus was appointed to the Robinson case, she asks why he cannot refuse it. He replies,

For a number of reasons. The main one is, if I didn't I couldn't hold up my head in this town. I couldn't represent this county in the legislature. I couldn't even tell you and Jem not to do something again . . . Scout, simply by the nature of the work, every lawyer gets at least one case in his lifetime that affects him personally. This one's mine, I guess.

He later tells his brother Jack, within Scout's hearing,

> "You know, I'd hoped to get through life without a case of this kind, but John Taylor pointed at me, and said, 'You're it.'"
> "Let this cup pass from you, eh?"
> "Right. But do you think I could face my children otherwise?"

Atticus realizes that he is defeated before he begins but that he must begin if he is to uphold his values. The legal system offers at least a *chance* of success. In contrast to the lynch mob in the dark, the court represents the light of reason. Scout and Jem, in their innocence, believe that the court is the structure in which Atticus can defeat the mad dog of irrationality and racism. Scout thinks, "With [Atticus's] infinite capacity for calming turbulent seas, he could make a rape case as dry as a sermon . . . . Our nightmare had gone with daylight, everything would come out all right."

In the trial, Atticus attempts to make the jury and the town see the incident from the perspectives of both Mayella Ewell and of Tom Robinson and, thus, to understand that Mayella's accusation is a lie born from fear, emotional need, ignorance and poverty. From Mayella Atticus elicits the story of a lonely young woman imprisoned in poverty by her father's alcoholism. The Ewells, "white trash," are as alienated from Maycomb as Tom Robinson. Yet in the squalor of Ewell life, there is one disjunctive sight: Mayella's geraniums, as carefully tended as those of Miss Maudie Atkinson. These represent Mayella's desire to escape the life she lives, but that escape is denied her both by her own nature and by the rigid caste system of Maycomb. Scout compares her to the half-black and half-white children of Dolphus Raymond:

> She was as sad, I thought, as what Jem called a mixed child: white people wouldn't have anything to do with her because she lived among pigs; Negroes wouldn't have anything to do with her because she was white . . . . Tom Robinson was probably the only person who was ever decent to her.

This decency is Tom Robinson's undoing. He is a black man who finds himself in the most dangerous of circumstances. He is accosted by a white woman, and whether he struggles with her or runs, he is guilty. What emerges before the astonished eyes of the court is that Tom Robinson could not have raped Mayella Ewell. The evidence, that she was beaten by someone left-handed, becomes moot when Tom Robinson faces the court and all see that "his left arm was fully twelve inches shorter than his right and hung dead at his side. It ended in a small shriveled hand, and from as far away as the balcony I could see that it was no use to him."

Mayella, when confronted with her obvious lie, falls back on her whiteness as her defense. Her father Bob had disrupted the court earlier when he testified that, through the window, "I seen that black nigger yonder ruttin' on my Mayella!" His language illustrates the assumption that blacks are uncontrollable animals—mad dogs who must be exterminated. Mayella falls back on the same argument. The caste system of Maycomb names, categorizes and limits her, just as it names, categorizes and limits Tom Robinson. The boundary between them is an absolutely rigid one. Maycomb defines Tom Robinson as nonhuman; thus, Mayella only has to appeal to her whiteness—that which makes her "one of us"—to be right:

> Suddenly Mayella became articulate. "I got somethin' to say ... an' then I ain't gonna say no more. That nigger yonder took advantage of me an' if you fine fancy gentlemen don't wanta do nothin' about it then you're all yellow stinkin' cowards, stinkin' cowards, the lot of you."

Scout says that "Atticus had hit her hard in a way that was not clear to me." His questions are the "Do you really think so?" They force her to face the truth of her self, but faced with that truth, she, angrily and stubbornly, falls back within the safety of the community ethos, leaving critique and compassion behind.

Tom Robinson's real crime is not the rape: it is that he shows himself to be more than the definition that Maycomb has created for him. Scout says that Tom is, in his way, as much a gentleman as her father. Indeed, Tom is convicted because he acts out Atticus's maxim and stands in another's shoes. When asked why he helped Mayella,

> Tom Robinson hesitated, searching for an answer.
> "Looked like she didn't have nobody to help her, like I says ... I felt right sorry for her, she seemed to try more'n the rest of 'em—"

"*You* felt sorry for *her*, you felt *sorry* for her?" Mr. Gilmer seemed ready to rise to the ceiling.

The witness realized his mistake and shifted uncomfortably in the chair. But the damage was done.

This is Tom Robinson's crime.

The real mad dog in Maycomb is the racism that denies the humanity of Tom Robinson. Atticus takes on that mad dog. When Atticus makes his summation to the jury, he literally bares himself to the jury's and the town's anger: he "unbuttoned his vest, unbuttoned his collar, loosened his tie, and took off his coat. He never loosened a scrap of his clothing until he undressed at bedtime, and to Jem and me, this was the equivalent of him standing before us stark naked." Atticus tells the jury that what has happened between Mayella Ewell and Tom Robinson is a crime because it violates the rigid code and social structure of Maycomb. Mayella, willfully breaking this code by kissing a black man, now has to put the evidence of her crime out of her sight, for truly to see Tom Robinson is to have to confront and to redefine herself: "of necessity she must put him away from her—he must be removed from her presence, from this world. She must destroy the evidence of her offense."

Atticus also appeals to the jury in the terms of his ethic. Arguing that the legal system is the place where community codes and caste systems must be left behind, he asks the jury to think rationally and critically, to ask themselves "Do you really think so?":

> A court is only as sound as its jury, and a jury is only as sound as the men who make it up. I am confident that you gentlemen will review *without passion* the evidence you have heard. . . . In the name of God, do your duty. (emphasis added)

He also asks them to acknowledge Tom Robinson's humanity, to have for Tom the compassion that Tom had for Mayella Ewell. Atticus finishes his argument with a prayer: "In the name of God, believe him."

This is not to be. As the town waits for the verdict, a sleepy Scout watches her father in the hot courtroom, and, in her thoughts, she binds the mad dog theme to Tom Robinson:

> But I must have been reasonably awake or I would not have received the impression that was creeping into me. It was not unlike one I had last winter, and I shivered, though the night was hot. The feeling grew until the atmosphere in the courtroom was

exactly the same as a cold February morning, when the mockingbirds were still, and the carpenters had stopped hammering on Miss Maudie's new house, and every wood door in the neighborhood was shut as tight as the doors of the Radley Place. A deserted waiting, empty street, and the courtroom was packed with people. A steaming summer night was no different from a winter morning. Mr. Heck Tate, who had entered the courtroom and was talking to Atticus might have been wearing his high boots and lumber jacket. Atticus had stopped his tranquil journey and had put his foot onto the bottom rung of a chair; as he listened to what Mr. Tate was saying, he ran his hand slowly up and down his thigh. I expected Mr. Tate to say any minute, "Take him, Mr. Finch . . ."

She continues, finding in the courtroom the images of Atticus's facing Tim Johnson, the mad dog, in the street:

What happened after that had a dreamlike quality: in a dream I saw the jury return, moving like underwater swimmers, and Judge Taylor's voice came from far away and was tiny. I saw something only a lawyer's child could be expected to see, could be expected to watch for, and it was like watching Atticus walk into the street, raise a rifle to his shoulder and pull the trigger, but watching all the time knowing that the gun was empty.

Though Tom Robinson is convicted, Atticus wins a small victory; the jury's deliberation lasts well into the night. Miss Maudie Atkinson confirms that Atticus' role is to face the mad dogs. He makes Maycomb question itself in a way no one else could, even though they, like Mayella, cannot bind love to power and act in creative justice.

"We're the safest folks in the world," said Miss Maudie. 'We're so rarely called on to be Christians, but when we are, we've got men like Atticus to go for us . . . . [As] I waited, I thought, Atticus Finch won't win, he can't win, but he's the only man in these parts who can keep a jury out so long in a case like that. And I thought to myself, well, we're making a step—it's just a baby step, but it's a step."

This baby step is not enough for Tom Robinson. He cannot trust that he can have justice, so he attempts to escape from prison and is shot dead in the attempt. This man who performed a loving act is treated like a rabid mad dog. The prison is a metaphor for Tom's position in the Maycomb of the 1930s. What is a baby step for the town is merely continuing oppression for Tom, the innocent man. Charles H. Long points out that, potentially, "passive power is still power. It is the power to be, to understand, to know even in the worst of historical circumstances, and it may often reveal a more clear insight into significant meaning of the human venture than the power possessed by the oppressor." This Tom Robinson cannot believe, so he cannot wait. His is the silence of the oppressed person who has reached despair.

Jem, moving into adulthood, also feels Tom's despair. Tom Robinson's conviction and his death mark Jem's fall from innocence; as he tells Miss Maudie, his life until now has been "like bein' a caterpillar in a cocoon. . . . Like somethin' asleep wrapped up in a warm place." Now, he must come to terms with what he has witnessed. Atticus tells Scout, who does not understand Jem's despair, that "Jem was trying hard to forget something, but what he was really doing was storing it away for a while. . . . When he was able to think about it, Jem would be himself again." Yet Jem is marked forever by the experience. Scout begins the novel by describing Jem's arm:

> When he was nearly thirteen, my brother Jem got his arm badly broken at the elbow. When it healed, and Jem's fears of never being able to play football were assuaged, he was seldom self-conscious about his injury. His left arm was somewhat shorter than his right; when he stood or walked, the back of his hand was at right angles to his body, his thumb parallel to his thigh.

Jem's arm, broken in his and Scout's "longest journey together," the night they survive Bob Ewell's vengeful attack, parallels Tom Robinson's withered arm, lost in a piece of machinery. Tom's lost arm and hand are ultimately crippling; they symbolize his inability to climb out of the prison of racism, his being crushed in its machinery. As Tom tries to escape, he is hindered by his loss: "They said if he'd had two good arms he'd have made it." Jem is crippled and lives; but, the injury is the sign of the experience's "leaving its mark" on Jem's body and on his soul.

Similarly, Boo Radley makes his mark on Scout. *To Kill A Mockingbird* is divided into two parts: the first is the children's attempt to make Boo Radley come out of his house, and the second is the trial of Tom Robinson. At first, the two seem unrelated; however, one soon realizes that Boo Radley is a hermeneutical device for the children's coming to understand the adult world represented by the rape trial. Like Tom Robinson, Boo Radley, who commits a childhood offense and is imprisoned by his family as punishment, is one of the least powerful members of Maycomb society. Parallel to Tom's trial, from which the truth about the community's racism emerges, is the children's attempt to see Boo Radley and to make him emerge from hiding.

Tom Robinson's trial and death make Jem realize that the very limited kind of communication that Boo has with him and Scout—for example, his leaving them gum and soap dolls in the knothole of a tree—is the only connection with the outside world that Boo can claim. Jem decides that, in a world in which a Tom Robinson is falsely accused and convicted and, finally, dies, Boo Radley does not *want* to come out. In Maycomb, there is no vital role for either Boo Radley or for Tom Robinson except as phantom and monster. For the disillusioned Jem, there is no longer a place for the childhood wonder that Boo represents. But in that mysterious role of ghost and phantom, Boo makes one powerful act as he emerges to save the children from Bob Ewell's attack.

Scout, too young to understand exactly what Tom Robinson's death means, does not lose her capacity for wonder. She sees Boo, and their meeting is Scout's rite of passage in the novel. Boo is the catalyst for the wonder that is the beginning of understanding. Scout and Jem's friend Dill sets in motion the children's investigation of the mystery of Boo Radley: "[H]e would wonder. 'Wonder what [Boo] does in there. . . . Wonder what he looks like.'" Scout, true to her name, enters this uncharted territory. She is willing to risk the exploration of the unknown, and her discovery is a profound one.

This risk almost causes her death. Bob Ewell, seeking revenge, attacks Jem and Scout as they walk home from a school play. Jem and Scout are saved by their mysterious phantom, Boo Radley, and Scout gets to see the man who has been the object of the children's speculations:

> His lips parted in a timid smile, and our neighbor's image blurred with my sudden tears.
> "Hey, Boo," I said.
> "Mr Arthur, honey," said Atticus gently correcting me.

This "grey ghost" that Scout desires to see appears and is given a name, and he gives Scout a gift beyond measure. As Scout walks Boo Radley home, she realizes that he, this "malevolent phantom," is her neighbor:

> Neighbors bring food with death and flowers with sickness and little things in between. Boo was our neighbor. He gave us two

soap dolls, a broken watch and chain, a pair of good-luck pennies, and our lives. But neighbors give in return. We never put back into the tree what we took out of it: we had given him nothing, and it made me sad.

What follows is both another gift from Boo and a gift to Boo; it is a gift that she will share with her wounded, sad brother and with us, the readers. Scout stands in Boo's shoes and sees the world and the turbulent events of this time from his front porch:

> I had never seen the neighborhood from this angle.
> . . . Atticus was right. One time he said you never really know a man until you stand in his shoes and walk around in them. Just standing on the Radley porch was enough . . .

Scout learns Atticus's ethic completely. Looking at her life from Boo's perspective, she is able to see herself and her experiences in a new way. This is the imaginative "Do you really think so?" and is the birth of Scout the writer and is the education of Scout the moral agent. She also makes an act of compassion—and this is her gift, as the neighbor, to Boo: she sees the world from his point of view and gains an understanding of him that no one else in Maycomb has ever had and, since he enters his house never to emerge again, ever will have. Scout looks into the face of the phantom and into Arthur Radley's human heart and realizes that her life and Boo's have been and are interrelated: that she is Boo's child as well as Atticus's, nurtured and protected by both to this moment. Maycomb had been told recently that "there was nothing to fear except fear itself," and Scout realizes the truth of this. She tells Atticus that "nothin's real scary except in books" and that Boo was "real nice." Atticus replies, "Most people are, Scout, when you finally see them."

Atticus, then, casts his ethic in visual terms, and in the metaphor of vision, the function and the content of the novel merge. In the preface to "The Nigger of the 'Narcissus,'" Joseph Conrad links compassion with vision and imagination with morality and makes clarity of vision the task of the artist. The artist, he says, creates community by appealing to the "human fellow feeling" that links us with all humankind:

> My task which I am trying to achieve is, by the power of the written word . . . to make you see. . . . If I succeed, you shall find there according to your deserts: encouragement, consolation, fear, charm . . . and, perhaps, also that glimpse of truth for which

you have forgotten to ask. . . . And when it is accomplished—
behold!—all the truth of life is there: a moment of vision, a sigh,
a smile—and the return to eternal rest.

The adult Scout telling us her story is the artist who grounds this call for
vision in a character: her father. She, in insisting with her father that seeing
is a hermeneutical act, gives us a true meeting with the "other" and brings us,
perhaps, to a moment of insight into our own lives, our own assumptions and
our own frailties. The work of art becomes, potentially, a moral and ethical
reference point, a pair of shoes in which we can stand.

   The deepest symbol in the novel is Atticus Finch himself. Atticus,
when he gives the children their air rifles, states the moral lesson of the
novel. He tells them that it is a sin to kill a mockingbird; that is, it is wrong
to do harm to something or to someone who only tries to help us or to give
us pleasure. That rule, combined with critical reflection on the self and with
compassion for others, keeps us from becoming mad dogs, from destroying
each other and, finally, ourselves. Scout understands this lesson as she, along
with sheriff Heck Tate and her father, agree that Boo should not be charged
for Bob Ewell's murder. When Atticus asks Scout if she understands this
adult decision, she responds: "Well, it'd be sort of like shootin' a mockingbird, wouldn't it?"

   Atticus stands at the novel's heart and as its moral and ethical center:
a man who knows himself and who, therefore, can love others. Scout
presents her father to us as a gift and a guide. She shows us a man who gives
up himself as he forces us to see and, thus, to know others by seeing
through him, yet he is far from being a "grey ghost." Atticus emerges
clearly, as a particular, ethical human being—as May Sarton's heroic,
decent man—but also as an enduring symbol of the good. Toni Morrison
calls such "timeless, benevolent, instructive, and protective" people "ancestors" because they so perfectly represent humanity that their wisdom tran-
scends their physical being. For Scout, the child as well as the artist, and
for us, because of her art, Atticus is ancestor, eternally present as comforter
and critic, as structure and source:

   He turned out the light and went into Jem's room. He would be
   there all night, and he would be there when Jem waked up in the
   morning.

DEAN SHACKELFORD

The Female Voice in To Kill a Mockingbird: Narrative Strategies in Film and the Novel

Aunt Alexandra was fanatical on the subject of my attire. I could not possibly hope to be a lady if I wore breeches; when I said I could do nothing in a dress, she said I wasn't supposed to be doing anything that required pants. Aunt Alexandra's vision of my deportment involved playing with small stoves, tea sets, and wearing the Add-A-Pearl necklace she gave me when I was born; furthermore, I should be a ray of sunshine in my father's lonely life. I suggested that one could be a ray of sunshine in pants just as well, but Aunty said that one had to behave like a sunbeam, that I was born good but had grown progressively worse every year. She hurt my feelings and set my teeth permanently on edge, but when I asked Atticus about it, he said there were already enough sunbeams in the family and to go about my business, he didn't mind me much the way I was.

This passage reveals the importance of female voice and gender issues in Harper Lee's popular Pulitzer Prize-winning novel, *To Kill a Mockingbird*, first published in 1960. The novel portrays a young girl's love for her father and brother and the experience of childhood during the Great Depression in a racist, segregated society which uses superficial and materialistic values to judge outsiders, including the powerful character Boo Radley.

From *Mississippi Quarterly* 50:1 (Winter 1996-97). © 1996 by Southeast Missouri State University.

In 1962, a successful screen version of the novel (starring Gregory Peck) appeared. However, the screenplay, written by Horton Foote, an accomplished Southern writer, abandons, for the most part, the novel's first-person narration by Scout (in the motion picture, a first-person angle of vision functions primarily to provide transitions and shifts in time and place). As a result, the film is centered more on the children's father, Atticus Finch, and the adult world in which Scout and Jem feel alien. As several commentators have noted, the film seems centered on the racial issue much more than on other, equally successful dimensions of the novel. Clearly, part of the novel's success has to do with the adult-as-child perspective. Lee, recalling her own childhood, projects the image of an adult reflecting on her past and attempting to recreate the experience through a female child's point of view.

That the film shifts perspectives from the book's primary concern with the female protagonist and her perceptions to the male father figure and the adult male world is noteworthy. While trying to remain faithful to the importance of childhood and children in the novel, Foote's objective narration is interrupted only occasionally with the first-person narration of a woman, who is presumably the older, now adult Scout. However, the novel is very much about the experience of growing up as a female in a South with very narrow definitions of gender roles and acceptable behavior. Because this dimension of the novel is largely missing from the film's narrative, the film version of *To Kill a Mockingbird* may be seen as a betrayal of the novel's full feminist implications—a compromise of the novel's full power.

Granted, when a film adaptation is made, the screenwriter need not be faithful to the original text. As Robert Giddings, Keith Selby, and Chris Wensley note in their important book *Screening the Novel*, a filmmaker's approaches to adapting a literary work may range from one of almost complete faithfulness to the story to one which uses the original as an outline for a totally different work on film. Foote's adaptation seems to fall somewhere in between these extremes, with the film decidedly faithful to certain aspects of the novel. His story clearly conveys the novel's general mood; it is obvious he wishes to remain close to the general subject matter of life in the South during the Great Depression and its atmosphere of racial prejudice and Jim Crow. Reflecting on the film, Harper Lee herself states, "For me, Maycomb is there, its people are there: in two short hours one lives a childhood and lives it with Atticus Finch, whose view of life was the heart of the novel."

Though admittedly Atticus Finch is at the heart of the film and novel, there are some clear and notable discrepancies between the two versions that alter the unique perspective of the novel considerably—despite what Lee herself has commented. Only about 15% of the novel is devoted to Tom

Robinson's rape trial, whereas in the film, the running time is more than 30% of a two-hour film. Unlike the book, the film is primarily centered on the rape trial and the racism of Maycomb which has made it possible—not surprising considering it was made during what was to become the turbulent period of the 1960s when racial issues were of interest to Hollywood and the country as a whole. Significant, though, are the reviewers and critics who believe this issue, rather than the female child's perspectives on an adult male world, is the novel's main concern and as a result admire the film for its faithfulness to the original.

Many teachers of the novel and film also emphasize this issue to the neglect of other equally important issues. In 1963 and again in the year of the film's twenty-fifth anniversary, the Education Department of Warner Books issued Joseph Mersand's study guide on the novel, one section of which is an essay subtitled "A Sociological Study in Black and White." Turning the novel into sociology, many readers miss other aspects of Lee's vision. In an early critical article Edgar Schuster notes that the racial dimensions of the novel have been overemphasized, especially by high school students who read it, and he offers possible strategies for teaching students the novel's other central issues, which he lists as "Jem's physiological and psychological growth" (mentioning Scout's growth in this regard only briefly as if it is a side issue), the caste system of Maycomb, the title motif, education, and superstition. What is so striking about Schuster's interpretation is his failure to acknowledge that the issue of Scout's gender is crucial to an understanding not only of the novel but also of Scout's identification with her father. As feminists often note, male readers sometimes take female perspectives and turn them into commentaries from a male point of view. Because the novel and film center so much on Atticus, he, rather than Scout, becomes the focus.

With regard to the film, I do not mean to suggest that Foote has not attempted to make some references to Scout's problems with gender identity. When he does, however, the audience is very likely unable to make the connections as adequately as careful readers of the novel might. Of particular interest are two scenes from the film which also appear in the novel. During one of their summers with Dill, Jem insults Scout as the three of them approach the Radley home and Scout whines, fearful of what may happen. As in the novel, he tells her she is getting to be more like a girl every day, the implication being that boys are courageous and non-fearful and girls are weak and afraid (a point which is refuted when Jem's fears of Boo Radley and the dark are demonstrated). Nevertheless, what is most important in the scene is Scout's reaction. Knowing that being called a girl is an insult and that being female is valued less than being male in her small Southern town, she suddenly becomes brave in order to remain acceptable to her brother.

In another scene, as Scout passes by Mrs. Dubose's house and says "hey," she is reprimanded for poor manners unbecoming of a Southern lady. This scene occurs in both film and novel. However, in the novel Lee clarifies that the presumed insult to Mrs. Dubose originates with Mrs. Dubose's assumptions as a Southern lady, a role which Scout, in the novel especially, is reluctant to assume. The film's lack of a consistent female voice makes this scene as well as others seem unnecessary and extraneous. This is only one example of the way in which the superior narrative strategy of the novel points out the weakness of the objective, male-centered narration of the film.

One scene from the film concerning girlhood does not appear in the novel. Careful not to suggest that the Finches are churchgoers (for what reason?), as they are in the novel, Foote creates a scene which attempts to demonstrate Scout's ambivalence about being female. As Scout becomes old enough to enter school, she despises the thought of wearing a dress. When she appears from her room to eat breakfast before attending school for the first time, Jem ridicules her while Atticus, Miss Maudie, and Calpurnia admire her. Scout comments: "I still don't see why I have to wear a darn old dress." A weakness of the film in this regard is that until this scene, there has been little indication that Scout strongly dislikes wearing dresses, let alone has fears of growing up as a female. The novel makes it clear that Scout prefers her overalls to wearing dresses, which is perhaps why Foote found it necessary to create this particular scene. However, the previous two crucial scenes, while faithful to the novel's general concerns with gender, create loose ends in the film which do not contribute to the success of the narration and which compromise the novel's feminist center.

The intermittent efforts to focus on the female narrator's perspective prove unsuccessful in revealing the work's feminist dimensions. As the film opens, the audience sees the hands of a small girl, presumably Scout, coloring. After the credits, a woman's voice, described by Amy Lawrence as a "disembodied voice exiled from the image," is heard reflecting on her perceptions of Maycomb. By introducing the audience to the social and spatial context, this first-person narrator provides a frame for the whole. The audience at this point, without having read the novel first, may not, however, recognize who the speaker is. As Scout appears playing in the yard, the viewer is left to assume that the voice-over opening the film is the female character speaking as a grown woman. The camera zooms down to reveal Scout and soon thereafter shifts to the standard objective narration of most films.

When the disembodied narrator is heard again, she reflects on Scout's views of Atticus after he insists she will have to return to school; yet, despite what her teacher says, father and daughter will continue reading each night the way they always have. Here the voice-over is designed to emphasize the heroic stature of Atticus and perhaps even to suggest that one reason for Scout's identification with him is his freedom of thought and action: "There just didn't seem to be anyone or thing Atticus couldn't explain. Though it wasn't a talent that would arouse the admiration of any of our friends. Jem and I had to admit he was very good at that but that was all he was good at, we thought." This intrusion becomes little more than a transition into the next scene, in which Atticus shoots the mad dog.

In the next intrusion the female voice interrupts the objective narration when, at school, Scout fights Cecil Jacobs for calling Atticus a "nigger lover." She states: "Atticus had promised me he would wear me out if he ever heard of me fightin' any more. I was far too old and too big for such childish things, and the sooner I learned to hold in, the better off everybody would be. I soon forgot. . . Cecil Jacobs made me forget." Here again, the first-person narration provides coherence, allowing the scene of Scout's fight with Cecil Jacobs to be shortened and placing emphasis on the relationship between Atticus and Scout. The subtext of their conversation could perhaps be viewed as a reflection of traditional views that women should not be too aggressive or physical, but this scene, coupled with earlier scenes reflecting social values, is not couched in terms of Scout's transgressive behavior as a woman-to-be. The female voice in the film is not used to demonstrate the book's concern with female identity; rather, it reinforces the male-centered society which Atticus represents and which the film is gradually moving toward in focusing on the trial of Tom Robinson.

Another instance during which the female narrator intrudes on the objective, male-centered gaze of the camera occurs when Jem and Scout discuss the presents Boo Radley leaves for them in the knot-hole. At this point in the film, the attempt to convey the book's female narrative center falls completely apart. Not until after the very long trial scene does the camera emphasize the children's perceptions or the female narrator's angle of vision again. Instead, the audience is in the adult male world of the courtroom, with mature male authority as the center of attention. Immediately after the trial, the film seems most concerned with Jem's reactions to the trial, Jem's recognition of the injustice of the verdict in the Tom Robinson case, and Jem's desire to accompany his father when he tells Helen Robinson that Tom has been killed. Scout is unable to observe directly the last event, and, as a result, the narration is inconsistent—by and large from the rape trial to the end of the film.

The film does, however make use of voice-over narration twice more. In the first instance, the female narrator again provides the transition in time and place to move from the previous scene, the revelation of Tom Robinson's death to his wife, into the confrontation between Atticus and Bob Ewell. As the camera focuses on an autumn scene with Scout dressed in a white dress, Jean Louise prepares the audience for the climax, which soon follows: "By October things had settled down again. I still looked for Boo every time I went by the Radley place. This night my mind was filled with Halloween. There was to be a pageant representing our county's agricultural products. I was to be a ham. Jem said he would escort me to the school auditorium. Thus began our longest journey together." Following this passage is the climactic scene, when Bob Ewell attacks Scout and Jem and Boo Radley successfully rescues them.

Shortly thereafter, the camera focuses on Scout's recognition of Boo as the protector and savior of Jem and her, and for the remainder of the film, the narration, arguably for the first time, is centered entirely on Scout's perception of the adult male world. She hears Heck Tate and Atticus debate over what to do about exposing the truth that Boo has killed Ewell while defending the children. The movement of the camera and her facial expression clearly indicate that Scout sees the meaning behind the adult's desires to protect Boo from the provincial Maycomb community which has marginalized him—and this scene signifies Scout's initiation into the world of adulthood.

As the film draws to a close, Scout, still in her overalls which will not be tolerated much longer in this society, walks Boo home. For the last time the audience hears the female voice:

> Neighbors bring food with death, and flowers with sickness, and little things in between. Boo was our neighbor. He gave us two soap dolls, a broken watch, and chain, a knife, and our lives. One time Atticus said you never really knew a man until you stood in his shoes and walked around in them. Just standin' on the Radley porch was enough . . . . The summer that had begun so long ago ended, another summer had taken its place, and a fall, and Boo Radley had come out. . . . I was to think of these days many times;—of Jem, and Dill and Boo Radley, and Tom Robinson . . . and Atticus. He would be in Jem's room all night. And he would be there when Jem waked up in the morning.

The film ends, when, through a window, Scout is seen climbing into Atticus's lap while he sits near Jem. The camera gradually moves leftward away from the two characters in the window to a long shot of the house. By the end, then, the film has shifted perspective back to the female voice, fully identified the narrator as the older Scout (Jean Louise), and focused on the center of Scout's existence, her father (a patriarchal focus). The inconsistent emphasis on Scout and her perceptions makes the film seem disjointed.

Noting the patriarchal center of the film, Amy Lawrence suggests the possibility for a feminist reading. She argues that the disembodied narrator —as well as the author, Harper Lee, and the characters of Scout and Mayella Ewell—provides a "disjointed subjectivity" on film which is characteristic of "the experience of women in patriarchy." Such "disjointed subjectivity" is, however, missing from the novel, which centers on Scout's perceptions of being female in a male-dominated South. The novel's female-centered narration provides an opportunity for Lee to comment on her own childlike perceptions as well as her recognition of the problems of growing up female in the South. The feminine voice, while present in the film, receives far too little emphasis.

In the novel the narrative voice allows readers to comprehend what the film does not explain. Though some critics have attacked Lee's narration as weak and suggested that the use of first person creates problems with perspective because the major participant, first-person narrator must appear almost in all scenes, the novel's consistent use of first person makes it much clearer than the film that the reader is seeing all the events through a female child's eyes. Once the children enter the courtroom in the film, the center of attention is the adult world of Atticus Finch and the rape trial—not, as the book is able to suggest, the children's perceptions of the events which unravel before them.

Although it is clear in the film that Scout is a tomboy and that she will probably grow out of this stage in her life (witness the very feminine and Southern drawl of the female narrator, who, though not seen, conveys the image of a conventional Southern lady), the film, which does not openly challenge the perspective of white heterosexuals (male or female) nearly to the degree the novel does, does not make Scout's ambivalence about being a female in an adult male world clear enough. Because the novel's narrative vision is consistently first person throughout and as a result focused on the older Scout's perceptions of her growing-up years, the female voice is unquestionably heard and the narration is focused on the world of Maycomb which she must inevitably enter as she matures.

Furthermore, a number of significant questions about gender are raised in the novel: Is Scout (and, by implication, all females) an outsider looking on an adult male world which she knows she will be unable to enter as she grows into womanhood? Is her identification with Atticus due not only to her love and devotion for a father but also to his maleness, a power and freedom she suspects she will not be allowed to possess within the confines of provincial Southern society? Or is her identification with Atticus due to his androgynous nature (playing the role of mother and father to her and demonstrating stereotypically feminine traits: being conciliatory, passive, tolerant, and partially rejecting the traditional masculine admiration for violence, guns, and honor)? All three of these questions may lead to possible, even complementary readings which would explain Scout's extreme identification with her father.

As in the passage quoted at the beginning of this essays, the novel focuses on Scout's tomboyishness as it relates to her developing sense of a female self. Also evident throughout the novel is Scout's devotion to her father's opinions. Atticus seems content with her the way she is; only when others force him to do so does he concern himself with traditional stereotypes of the Southern female. Especially significant with regard to Scout's growing sense of womanhood is the novel's very important character, Aunt Alexandra, Atticus's sister, who is left out of the film entirely. Early in the novel, readers are made aware of Scout's antipathy for her aunt, who wishes to mold her into a Southern lady. Other female authority figures with whom Scout has difficulty agreeing are her first-grade teacher, Miss Fisher, and Calpurnia, the family cook, babysitter, and surrogate mother figure. When the females in authority interfere with Scout's perceptions concerning her father and their relationship, she immediately rebels, a rebellion which Atticus does not usually discourage—signifying her strong identification with male authority and her recognition that the female authority figures threaten the unique relationship which she has with her father and which empowers her as an individual.

Exactly why Scout identifies with Atticus so much may have as much to do with his own individuality and inner strength as the fact that he is a single parent and father. Since the mother of Scout and Jem is dead, Atticus has assumed the full responsibility of playing mother and father whenever possible—though admittedly he employs Calpurnia and allows Alexandra to move in with them to give the children, particularly Scout, a female role model. However, Atticus is far from a stereotypical Southern male. Despite his position as a respected male authority figure in Maycomb, he seems oblivious to traditional expectations concerning masculinity (for himself) and femininity (for Scout). The children in fact see him as rather unmanly: "When Jem and I asked him why he was so old, he said he got started late, which we felt reflected on his abilities and his masculinity." Jem is also upset because Atticus will not play tackle football. Mrs. Dubose criticizes Atticus for not remarrying, which is very possibly a subtle comment on his lack of virility. Later the children learn of his abilities at marksmanship, at bravery in watching the lynch mob ready to attack Tom Robinson, and at the defense of the same man. Perhaps this is Lee's way of suggesting that individuals must be allowed to develop their own sense of self without regard to rigid definitions of gender and social roles.

Scout's identification with Atticus may also be rooted in her recognition of the superficiality and limitations of being a Southern female. Mrs. Dubose once tells her: "'You should be in a dress and camisole, young lady! You'll grow up waiting on tables if somebody doesn't change your ways . . .'" This is one of many instances in the novel through which the first-person narrator reveals Lee's criticism of Southern women and their narrowmindedness concerning gender roles. Even Atticus ridicules the women's attitudes. In one instance he informs Alexandra that he favors "'Southern womanhood as much as anybody, but not for preserving polite fiction at the expense of human life.'" When Scout is "indignant" that women cannot serve on juries, Atticus jokingly says, "I guess it's to protect our frail ladies from sordid cases like Tom's. Besides . . . I doubt if we'd ever get a complete case tried—the ladies'd be interrupting to ask questions.'" This seemingly sexist passage may in fact be the opposite; having established clearly that Atticus does not take many Southern codes seriously, Lee recognizes the irony in Atticus's statement that women, including his own independent-minded daughter, are "frail."

Admittedly, few women characters in the novel are very pleasant, with the exceptions of Miss Maudie Atkinson, the Finches' neighbor, and Calpurnia. Through the first-person female voice, Southern women are ridiculed as gossips, provincials, weaklings, extremists, even racists—calling to mind the criticism of Southern manners in the fiction of Flannery O'Connor. Of Scout's superficial Aunt Alexandra, Lee writes: ". . . Aunt Alexandra was one of the last of her kind: she has river-boat, boardingschool manners; let any moral come along and she would uphold it; she was born in the objective case; she was an incurable gossip." Scout's feelings for Alexandra, who is concerned with family heritage, position, and conformity to traditional gender roles, do alter somewhat as she begins to see Alexandra as a woman who means well and loves her and her father, and as she begins to accept certain aspects of being a Southern female. As Jem and Dill exclude her from their games, Scout gradually learns more about the alien world of being a female through sitting on the porch with Miss Maudie and observing Calpurnia work in the kitchen, which makes her begin "to think there was more skill involved in being a girl" than she has previously thought. Nevertheless, the book makes it clear that the adult Scout, who narrates the novel and who has presumably now assumed the feminine name Jean Louise for good, is still ambivalent at best concerning the traditional Southern lady.

Of special importance with regard to Scout's growing perceptions of herself as a female is the meeting of the missionary society women, a scene which, like Aunt Alexandra's character, is completely omitted from the film. Alexandra sees herself as a grand host. Through observing the missionary women, Scout, in Austenian fashion, is able to satirize the superficialities and prejudices of Southern women with whom she is unwilling to identify in order to become that alien being called woman. Dressed in "my pink Sunday dress, shoes, and a petticoat," Scout attends a meeting shortly after Tom Robinson's death, knowing that her aunt makes her participate as "part of . . . her campaign to teach me to be a lady." Commenting on the women, Scout says, "Rather nervous, I took a seat beside Miss Maudie and wondered why ladies put on their hats to go across the street. Ladies in bunches always filled me with vague apprehension and a firm desire to be elsewhere . . ."

As the meeting begins, the ladies ridicule Scout for frequently wearing pants and inform her that she cannot become a member of the elite, genteel group of Southern ladyhood unless she mends her ways. Miss Stephanie Crawford, the town gossip, mocks Scout by asking her if she wants to grow up to be a lawyer, a comment to which Scout, coached by Aunt Alexandra, says, "Nome, just a lady"—with the obvious social satire evident. Scout clearly does not want to become a lady. Suspicious, Miss Stephanie replies, "Well, you won't get very far until you start wearing dresses more often.'" Immediately thereafter, Lee exposes even further the provincialism and superficiality of the group's appearance of gentility, piety, and morality. Mrs. Grace Meriwether's comments on "'those poor Mruna'" who live "'in that jungle'" and need Christian salvation reflect a smug, colonialist attitude toward other races. When the women begin conversing about blacks in America, their bigotry—and Scout's disgust with it—becomes obvious.

Rather than the community of gentility and racism represented in the women of Maycomb, Scout clearly prefers the world of her father, as this passage reveals: " . . . I wondered at the world of women . . . . There was no doubt about it, I must soon enter this world, where on its surface fragrant ladies rocked slowly, fanned gently, and drank cool water." The female role is far too frivolous and unimportant for Scout to identify with. Furthermore, she says, "But I was more at home in my father's world. People like Mr. Heck Tate did not trap you with innocent questions to make fun of you. . . . Ladies seemed to live in faint horror of men, seemed unwilling to approve whole-heartedly of them. But I liked them . . . . [N]o matter how undelectable they were, . . . they weren't hypocrites.'" This obviously idealized and childlike portrayal of men nevertheless gets at the core of Scout's conflict. In a world in which men seem to have the advantages and seem to be more fairminded and less intolerant than women with their petty concerns and superficial dress codes, why should she conform to the notion of Southern ladyhood? Ironically, Scout, unlike the reader, is unable to recognize the effects of female powerlessness which may be largely responsible for the attitudes of Southern ladies. If they cannot control the everyday business and legal affairs of their society, they can at least impose their code of manners and morality.

To Scout, Atticus and his world represent freedom and power. Atticus is the key representative of the male power which Scout wishes to obtain even though she is growing up as a Southern female. More important, Lee demonstrates that Scout is gradually becoming a feminist in the South, for, with the use of first-person narration, she indicates that Scout/Jean Louise still maintains the ambivalence about being a Southern lady she possessed as a child. She seeks to become empowered with the freedoms the men in her society seem to possess without question and without resorting to trivial and superficial concerns such as wearing a dress and appearing genteel.

Harper Lee's fundamental criticism of gender roles for women (and to a lesser extent for men) may be evident especially in her novel's identification with outsider figures such as Tom Robinson, Mayella Ewell, and Boo Radley. Curiously enough, the outsider figures with whom the novelist identifies most are also males. Tom Robinson, the male African American who has been disempowered and annihilated by a fundamentally racist, white male society, and Boo Radley, the reclusive and eccentric neighbor about whom legends of his danger to the fragile Southern society circulate regularly, are the two "mockingbirds" of the title. Ironically, they are unable to mock society's roles for them and as a result take the consequences of living on the margins—Tom, through his death; Boo, through his return to the protection of a desolate isolated existence.

Throughout the novel, however, the female voice has emphasized Scout's growing distance from her provincial Southern society and her identification with her father, a symbol of the empowered. Like her father, Atticus, Scout, too, is unable to be a "mockingbird" of society and as a result, in coming to know Boo Radley as a real human being at novel's end, she recognizes the empowerment of being the other as she consents to remain an outsider unable to accept society's unwillingness to seek and know before it judges. And it is perhaps this element of the female voice in Harper Lee's *To Kill a Mockingbird* which most makes Horton Foote's screen adaptation largely a compromise of the novel's full power.

Chronology

1926   Nelle Harper Lee born April 28 in Monroeville, Alabama, the youngest of three daughters of Amasa Coleman (A.C.) Lee and Frances Fincher Lee. Her father was a lawyer, publisher of the Monroe Journal, and had served as a state senator.

1931–42   Attends public schools in Monroeville. Truman Capote lives next door during the summers and the two remain friends until his death in 1984. The character of Dill in *To Kill a Mockingbird* will be modeled upon Capote. Lee will be a partial model for the character of Idabell in Capote's *Other Voices, Other Rooms*.

1944–45   Attends Huntington College, Montgomery, Alabama.

1945–50   Studies law at the University of Alabama, as her father had done, but does not complete degree.

1949–50   Studies for one year at Oxford University, then moves to New York City.

1951   Mother dies.

1950s   Works as reservation clerk with Eastern Air Lines and British Overseas Airways, New York.

1957   Approaches literary agent with two essays and three short stories, one of which will be expanded to become her only novel, *To Kill a Mockingbird*. Encouraged by Lipincott editor Tay Hohoff, quits airlines to devote full time to writing.

1959   Accompanies Truman Capote to Holcomb, Kansas, to help research his book *In Cold Blood*.

1960   Eight years in preparation, *To Kill a Mockingbird* is published; remains on best-seller list for eighty weeks; soon translated into ten languages; Literary Guild and Book-of-the-Month Club selection, Reader's Digest Condensed Book, published in paperback by Popular Library.

1961   Awarded Pulitzer Prize for Fiction; first woman to do so since 1942. Receives Alabama Library Association award, and Brotherhood Award of National Conference of Christians and Jews. "Christmas Me" published in December issue of *McCall's*; "Love—In Other Words" published in April issue of *Vogue*. Father dies.

1962   Horton Foote writes screenplay of *To Kill a Mockingbird*; produced as film by Universal Studios. Novel receives *Best Sellers'* Paperback of the Year Award.

1966–72   Member, National Council on the Arts.

1987   *To Kill a Mockingbird* adapted as London stage play by Christopher Sergel.

1987–
present   Harper Lee lives in New York City, returning each winter to Monroeville, Alabama, to stay with her older sister, Alice Lee. She famously continues to live as a recluse, refusing all interviews and awards.

1995   Thirty-fifth anniversary edition of *To Kill a Mockingbird* published.

1997   30 million copies of *To Kill a Mockingbird* in print; translated into forty languages.

Contributors

HAROLD BLOOM is Sterling Professor of Humanities at Yale University and Professor of English at New York University. His works include *Shelley's Mythmaking* (1959), *The Visionary Company* (1961), *The Anxiety of Influence* (1973), *Agon: Towards a Theory of Revisionism* (1982), *The Book of J* (1990), *The American Religion* (1992), and *The Western Canon* (1994). His forthcoming books are a study of Shakespeare and *Freud, Transference and Authority*, which considers all of Freud's major writings. A MacArthur Prize Fellow, Professor Bloom is the editor of more than thirty anthologies and general editor of five series of literary criticism published by Chelsea House.

HARDING LEMAY is a critic and writer for television. His works include *Eight Years in Another World* (1981) and *Inside, Looking Out; a Personal Memoir* (1971), and numerous articles and reviews in newspapers and magazines.

GRANVILLE HICKS, born in 1901, is a Marxist literary critic and author. He has written introductions for several volumes, including John Reed's *Ten Days that Shook the World* (1935). His volumes include *The Great Tradition; an Interpretation of American Literature Since the Civil War* (1967), and *Figures of Transition; a Study of British Literature at the End of the Nineteenth Century* (1939). He is the author of several works of fiction, including the utopian novel *The First to Awaken* (1940).

EDGAR H. SCHUSTER was for many years a high school teacher and a writer-editor at a major publishing company. He has written articles on

American literature and is author of the series for young readers *Words Are Important* (1985, 1979); *Grammar, Usage, and Style* (1965); and *A Modern Approach to Language Study* (1961).

EDWIN BRUELL is former Chair of the English Department at Bremen High School, Midlothian, Illinois.

CLAUDIA DURST JOHNSON is Professor of English at the University of Alabama. She is author of *An Annotated Bibliography of Shakespearean Burlesques, Parodies, and Travesties* (1976) *American Actress: Perspectives on the Nineteenth Century* (1984), *To Kill a Mockingbird: Threatening Boundaries* (1994), and the forthcoming *Understanding the Scarlet Letter* and *Huckleberry Finn* in the "Literature in Context" series.

FRED ERISMAN is co-editor, with Richard W. Etulain, of *Fifty Western Writers: a Bio-bibliographical Sourcebook* (1982) and author of volumes on Laura Ingalls Wilder (1994), Tony Hillerman (1989), and Frederick Remington (1975), in the Boise State University Western Writers Series.

WILLIAM T. GOING is author of *Scanty Plot of Ground: Studies in the Victorian Sonnet* (1976) and *Essays on Alabama Literature* (1975).

COLIN NICHOLSON is Senior Lecturer in English Literature at Edinburgh University. He has published widely on Scottish, American, Canadian, and English literature. His most current works are *Ian Crichton Smith: New Critical Essays* and *Landscapes of the Mind*.

CAROLYN M. JONES is an assistant professor of religious studies and English at Louisiana State University, where she also teaches in the university's Honors College. Her articles and essays have appeared in journals such as *Literature and Theology* and *African American Review*.

Bibliography

Childress, Mark. "Looking for Harper Lee." *Southern Living* 32:5 (May 1997): 148–50.

Contemporary Literary Criticism. Volume 12, 1980. Volume 60, 1990. Detroit: Gale.

Dictionary of Literary Biography, Volume 6: *American Novelists since World War II.* Detroit: Gale, 1980.

Johnson, Claudia Durst. *To Kill a Mockingbird: Threatening Boundaries.* New York: Twayne, 1994.

Moates, Marianne M. *A Bridge of Childhood: Truman Capote's Southern Years.* New York: Holt, 1989.

Montgomery, Leigh. "Harper Lee Still Prizes Privacy Over Publicity." *The Christian Science Monitor* (September 11, 1997):
http://scmonitor.com/durable/1997/09/11/feat/feat.3.html

Reviews of *To Kill a Mockingbird:*
    America (May 11, 1991): 509–11.
    Atlanta Constitution (May 25, 1993): A11.
    Atlanta Journal & Constitution (May 29, 1988): A2; (August 26, 1990): M1.
    Atlantic Monthly (August 1960): 98–99.
    Booklist (September 1, 1960).
    Chicago Sunday Tribune (July 17, 1960): 1.
    Christian Science Monitor (October 3, 1961): 6.
    Commonweal (December 9, 1960): 289.
    Item (March 3, 1991): 24.
    New Statesman (October 15, 1960): 580.
    Newsweek (January 9, 1961): 83.
    New Yorker (September 10, 1960).
    New York Herald Tribune (May 3, 1961): 16.
    New York Herald Tribune Book Review (July 10, 1960): 5.
    New York Times (June 6, 1993): 1.

Skube, Michael. "Searching for Scout." *The Atlanta Journal and Constitution* (1995):
http://www.yall.com/thearts/quill/harper.html

Acknowledgments

"Children Play; Adults Betray" by Harding LeMay from *New York Herald Tribune Book Review*, July 10, 1960, p. 5. Reprinted in *Contemporary Literary Criticism*, Volume 60. Copyright © 1960 by Harding LeMay.

"Three at the Outset" by Granville Hicks from *Saturday Review* XLIII:30 (July 23, 1960): 15–16. Reprinted in *Contemporary Literary Criticism*, Volume 60. Copyright © 1960 by Granville Hicks.

"Discovering Theme and Structure in *To Kill a Mockingbird*" by Edgar H. Schuster from *English Journal*, 52:7 (1963): 506–11. Copyright © 1963 by the National Council of Teachers of English.

"Keen Scalpel of Racial Ills" by Edwin Bruell from *English Journal* 53:9 (December 1964): 658–61. Copyright © 1964 by the National Council of Teachers of English.

"A Censorship Attempt in Hanover, Virginia, 1966" by Claudia Durst Johnson from *Understanding To Kill a Mockingbird: A Student Casebook to Issues, Sources, and Historic Documents* by Claudia Durst Johnson. Copyright © 1994 by Claudia Durst Johnson.

"The Romantic Regionalism of Harper Lee" by Fred Erisman from *The Alabama Review* XXVI:2 (April 1973): 122–36. Copyright © 1973 by The University of Alabama Press.

"*To Kill a Mockingbird*: Harper Lee's Tragic Vision" by R.A. Dave from *Indian Studies in American Fiction*, edited by M.K. Naik, S.K. Desai, and S. Mokashi-Punekar. Copyright © 1974 by The Macmillan Company of India Limited.

"Store and Mockingbird: Two Pulitzer Novels about Alabama" by William T. Going from *Essays on Alabama Literature*. Copyright © 1975 by William T. Going.

Index

Adams, Phoebe, 64
Adventures of Huckleberry Finn, The
   (Twain), 18–19, 39
Alexandra, Aunt, 12, 20, 44, 63, 84
  class and, 83
  code of, 71, 74
  family and, 42, 83
  Scout Finch and, 70, 74, 122, 123,
   124
  humor and, 55
  missionary circle of, 9, 20
  as old aristocracy, 41–42
  portrayal of, 123
  as teacher, 10
Anderson, Maxwell, 19
Aristotle, 58
Arthur, Mr., 63, 64
As You Like It (Shakespeare), 1–2
Atkinson, Maudie. *See* Maudie, Miss
"Atticus Finch and the Mad Dog:
  Harper Lee's *To Kill a
  Mockingbird*" (Jones), 99–113
Austen, Jane, 56, 57, 124
Autobiography, *To Kill a Mockingbird*
  as, 51–52, 68, 116, 121

Baldwin, James, 18, 102–3
Bernstein, Elmer, 95
Bloom, Harold, 1–2
Bruell, Edwin, 17–22, 44
Buck, Pearl S., 18
Burrell, Edwin, 102

Caldwell, Erskine, 20
Calpurnia, 5, 10, 20, 41, 50, 54, 84, 95,
  122, 123
  children and, 73
  film and, 91
  growth of Jem and, 12
  humanity of, 55
  law and, 69, 81
  as teacher, 10
Capote, Truman, 3, 63
Caroline, Miss, 10, 63, 66
Cash, W. J., 39
Caste system, of Maycomb, 9, 20,
  40–43, 107
Censorship, of *To Kill a Mockingbird*,
  23–38
"Censorship Attempt in Hanover,
  Virginia, 1966, A" (Johnson),
  23–38
Childhood, *To Kill a Mockingbird* and,
  3–4, 5, 52, 61–66, 121
  film and, 92–93, 116, 118, 121
  law and, 61–66
Children, 53–54
  See also Finch, Jem, Finch, Scout;
   Harris, Dill
"Children Play; Adults Betray"
  (Lemay), 3–4
Class structure, of South, 41–43, 83
  See also Caste system
Codes, law *versus*, 67–77, 80–81
Conrad, Joseph, 105, 112–13
Courthouse, in Maycomb, 40, 43, 87

Crawford, Stephanie, 55, 124
Cry, the Beloved Country (Paton), *To Kill a Mockingbird versus*, 17–22
Cunningham, Mr., 63, 103–4
  film and, 93–94
  Scout Finch and, 94–95
  law and, 81
Cunningham, Walter, 42, 45, 63, 72, 73
  Atticus Finch and, 44, 83–84
  law and, 69

Dave, R.A., 49–58
David Copperfield (Dickens), 51–52
Davis, Allison, 42
Dickens, Charles, 51–52, 57
Difference, people of as theme, 79–80
  See also Outsiders
"Discovering Theme and Structure in the Novel" (Schuster), 7–15
Dollard, John, 41
Dubose, Mrs., 8, 11, 15, 55, 62, 70, 84
  camelias of, 87
  candy episode and, 12
  Atticus Finch and, 84
  Scout Finch and, 118, 123
  as ghost, 11, 12
  Ivanhoe read to, 39–40
  Jem and, 65
  as outsider, 80, 85
  seclusion of, 20–21

Education, 9–10, 15, 47–48
  code of, 75–76
  film and, 90–91
  Scout Finch and, 70, 80
  law and, 69
Emerson, Ralph Waldo, *To Kill a Mockingbird*'s Southern Romanticism and, 39–48
Erisman, Fred, 39–48, 102, 103
Evans, Mrs., 75–76
Everett, J. Grimes, 9
Ewell, Bob, 8, 20, 21, 84

  as evil, 21, 53, 56, 70, 71, 73, 76
  film and, 93, 120
  Finch children attacked by, 63, 110, 111
  Atticus Finch *versus*, 73
  Hitler and, 70
  law and, 69, 70
  as outsider, 80, 85
  as poor white trash, 41
  Boo Radley killing, 47, 63, 77, 81, 98, 111, 113, 120
  trial and, 107
Ewell, Burris, 63
Ewell, Mayella, 20, 41, 56, 61, 70, 75, 84, 101, 103
  film and, 121
  Scout Finch *versus*, 73, 106
  as outsider, 80, 125
  trial and, 106, 107–8, 109

Family, *To Kill a Mockingbird* and, 42, 83, 90, 91
Faulkner, William, 20, 55, 57, 61, 63, 66
"Female Voice in *To Kill a Mockingbird*: Narrative Strategies in Film and the Novel, The" (Shackleford), 115–25
Feminist voice, in *To Kill a Mockingbird* book and film, 115–25
Film version. *See To Kill a Mockingbird* (film)
Finch, Alexandra. *See* Alexandra, Aunt
Finch, Atticus, 3, 4, 5, 10, 15, 20, 21, 84
  code of, 72–73
  as crusader, 21
  as Emersonian hero, 44–46, 102
  Bob Ewell *versus*, 73
  film and, 90, 92, 96, 97, 116
  Jem Finch and, 122
  Scout Finch and, 105, 113, 116, 117, 118–19, 120–23, 124–25
  as gentleman, 54, 84
  as Greek rational hero, 102

guns and, 87
as ideogram, 1
Jem's bad arm and, 11
language of, 82
law and, 67, 69, 70, 71, 74, 77
lynch mob and, 77, 103–4
mad dog killed by, 8, 50, 87, 90,
    100–101
missionary society and, 75
mockingbird and, 49, 86, 113
morality of, 99–113
Negroes and, 72, 82–83, 94
New South and, 43–46
as outsider, 80, 85
paternalism of, 83–84
Boo Radley and, 62, 77
as saint, 71–72, 77
as Southern liberal, 66
as teacher, 10
as tragic hero, 72
trial and, 41, 44, 45–46, 54, 57–58,
    61, 62, 63, 72, 74, 96–97, 101–2,
    102, 103, 105–9
women's attitudes and, 123
Finch, Jem, 3, 5, 70, 84
broken arm of, 11, 110
camelias of Mrs. Dubose and, 87
education and, 10
Bob Ewell and, 110, 111
film and, 92, 119
Atticus Finch and, 122
growth of, 12, 62, 63, 64, 65, 99, 100,
    101, 110
law and, 69, 71, 73, 74, 76, 81
as main character, 90
Maycomb and, 73
as mockingbird, 92
Negro church and, 55
as outsider, 79–80, 85
perception of truth of, 45
portrayal of, 53–54
Boo Radley and, 96, 98, 100, 110,
    111, 117
superstition and, 10
symbolism of name, 56
trial and, 54, 56, 63, 71, 73, 100, 106,

108, 110, 111
Finch, Scout, 3, 84
Aunt Alexandra and, 74, 122, 123,
    124
Calpurnia and, 122
Mr. Cunningham and, 94–95
Mrs. Dubose and, 118, 123
education and, 9–10, 14, 47–48, 70,
    75–76, 80
equal justice and, 79
Bob Ewell and, 110, 111
Mayella Ewell versus, 73, 106
film and, 90, 116, 117–22, 125
Atticus Finch and, 105, 113, 116, 117,
    118–19, 120–23, 124–25
Miss Fisher and, 122
gender identity and, 116, 117,
    118–19, 121–25
growth of, 14, 62, 63–66, 99, 101,
    111–12, 120
Dill Harris and, 70
law and, 69, 71, 72–73, 74, 81
as Harper Lee, 51–52, 68, 116, 121
Lee's straying from viewpoint of, 5
lynch mob and, 103–4
missionary society and, 80, 123–24
mockingbird and, 87, 113
naiveté of, 20
Negro church and, 55
as outsider, 70, 79–80, 80, 85, 125
point of view of, 64–66, 82, 90
portrayal of, 1–2, 19, 53–54
Boo Radley and, 83, 96, 98, 100,
    110–12, 117, 120, 125
superstition and, 10
symbolism of name, 56
as tomboy, 72, 80
trial and, 54, 56, 63, 71, 100, 106,
    107, 108–9
Finch, Simon, 53, 66
Fire, symbolism of, 52
"Fire and Ice" (Frost), 52
Fisher, Carolyn, 20, 47, 122
Foote, Horton, 116, 117, 118, 125
Freud, Sigmund, 58
Frost, Robert, 52

Gates, Miss, 10, 91
Ghosts, 11, 14–15
Giddings, Robert, 116
Gill, Brendon, 97
Going, William T., 61–66
Good Earth, The (Buck), 18
Gordon, Caroline, 61
Grapes of Wrath, The (Steinbeck), 18
Growth, of children, 14, 61–66, 90
   Jem Finch and, 9, 12, 62, 63, 64, 65,
     99, 100, 101, 110
   Scout Finch and, 14, 62, 63–66, 99,
     101, 111–12, 120
Guns, symbolism of, 87

Halloween episode, 63–64
Harris, Dill, 50, 62, 70, 84, 90, 111
   film and, 91
   Jem's bad arm and, 11
   naiveté of, 20
   as outsider, 85
   portrayal of, 53–54
   superstition and, 10
Hawthorne, Nathaniel, 76
Hemingway, Ernest, 18, 57
Hicks, Granville, 5, 64
Hitler, Adolf, 51, 70, 72, 76, 83
"Hollywood and Race: *To Kill a Mock-*
   ingbird" (Nicholson), 89–98
Humor, in *To Kill a Mockingbird*,
   54–55, 2057

Intruder in the Dust (Faulkner), 61
Ivanhoe (Scott), 39–40

Jacobs, Cecil, 119
James, Henry, 65
Johnson, Claudia Durst, 23–38, 67–87
Johnson, Tim, 101, 109
Jones, Carolyn, 99–113
Joseph K, 54
Joyce, James, 51–52
"Keen Scalpel on Racial Ills" (Bruell),
   17–22
King, Martin Luther, Jr., 77, 102–3,
   105
Ku Klux Klan, 42, 76

Lamb, Charles, 61, 69, 81
Law
   childhood and, 61–66
   codes *versus*, 67–77, 80–81
   Maycomb and, 98
Lawrence, Amy, 118, 121
Lee, Harper
   on censorship of *To Kill a Mockingbird*,
     37–38
   on film, 116
   as Scout Finch, 51–52, 68, 116, 121
Lemay, Harding, 3–4
Levy, Sam, 42
"Literary Analysis: Unifying Elements
   of *To Kill a Mockingbird*"
   (Johnson), 79–87
Long, Charles H., 110
Lost in the Stars (Anderson), 19
Lula, 55
Lyell, F. H., 64

McCullers, Carson, 1–2, 3, 63
MacIntyre, Alasdair, 102
Mad dog
   citizens of Maycomb as, 101–2, 103–4
   Atticus Finch shooting, 8, 50, 87, 90,
     100–101
   Tom Robinson as, 109–10
   trial as, 105–9
Maudie, Miss, 8, 49, 62, 84, 110, 123
   Atticus Finch and, 72
   fire and, 100
   humanity of, 55–56, 62
   law and, 69, 70
   mockingbird and, 86
   as outsider, 85
   trial and, 109
Maycomb, 51, 71
   caste system of, 9, 20, 40–43, 107

church in, 41
courthouse of, 40, 43, 87
film and, 93, 117
Scout Finch's perception of, 65
law and codes of, 67–77, 80–81, 98
loss of insulation of, 46–48
as microcosm of South, 40–43, 53,
    56–57, 59, 103
Negro church in, 55
Underwood's disdain of, 21
Merriweather, Mrs., 63, 75, 124
Mersand, Joseph, 117
Missionary society, 9, 20, 21, 41, 42,
    71, 83, 123–24
codes of, 74–75
Scout Finch and, 69, 80
Mockingbird, 21, 49–51, 52
film and, 91–92
Atticus Finch as, 65, 113
Jem Finch as, 92
Scout Finch as, 113
Finch family as, 56
imagery of, 86–87
Negro as, 51
Boo Radley as, 65, 81, 86–87, 125
Tom Robinson as, 9, 21, 50, 65, 81,
    86, 92, 125
Morality, To Kill a Mockingbird and,
    56–57, 58
equivocal nature of, 89–98
of Atticus Finch, 99–113
Morrison, Toni, 113
Mrunas, 9, 20, 75, 76, 124
Mulligan, Robert, 89, 91, 97
Mumford, Lewis, 46
Murdoch, Iris, 105

New South, 43–46
Nicholson, Colin, 89–98
"Nigger of the 'Narcissus,' The"
    (Conrad), 112–13

O'Connor, Flannery, 1, 123
Old Sarum, 71, 73, 76, 84

"Out of the Cradle Endlessly Rocking"
    (Whitman), 50–51
Outsiders, 83, 85, 125
differences and, 79–80
Atticus Finch as, 80, 85
Jem Finch as, 79–80, 85
Scout Finch as, 70, 79–80, 80, 85, 125
Dill Harris as, 85
Miss Maudie as, 85
Boo Radley as, 21, 70, 79–80, 85, 125
Tom Robinson as, 79–80, 125

Paton, Alan, Cry, the Beloved Country,
    17–22
Peck, Gregory, 90, 94, 96, 116
Poe, Edgar Allan, 66
Portrait of the Artist as a Young Man, A
    (Joyce), 51–52

Race prejudice issue, 3–4, 5, 8, 10–11,
    12, 15, 20, 21–22, 41, 51, 55, 58,
    63, 74, 75, 76, 83–84, 89, 101,
    108, 117
Radley, Boo, 3, 8, 11, 14, 15, 21, 47,
    50, 55, 62, 84, 101
children and, 62, 73, 96, 98, 100,
    110–11, 117
equal justice and, 79
Bob Ewell killed by, 77, 81, 98, 111,
    120
film and, 92, 95–96, 120
Scout Finch and, 83, 110–12, 125
humanity of, 62, 63–64
innocence of, 52–53, 56, 58
Jem's bad arm and, 11
law and, 81
as mockingbird, 65, 81, 86–87, 125
as outsider, 21, 70, 79–80, 85, 125
Tom Robinson and, 110–11
symbolism of, 95, 96
Radley house, 8, 11, 50, 58
film and, 92, 95–96
Radley, Nathan, 92
Rape, as censorship issue, 23–38

Raymond, Dolphus, 45, 70, 84, 106
  drunken facade of, 21
  as outsider, 85
Religious hypocrisy, 90, 91
  See also Missionary society
Robinson, Helen, 75, 119
Robinson, Tom, 7, 12, 19–20, 47, 63,
    83, 84
  children and, 10
  conviction of, 41
  equal justice and, 79
  escape and death of, 22, 58, 109–10
  film and, 92, 93, 96, 97, 117, 119
  Atticus Finch and, 44, 83
  innocence of, 52–53, 55–56, 57–58
  law and, 81
  lost arm of, 107, 110
  lynch-mob and, 77, 94–95, 103–4
  as mad dog, 109–10
  as mockingbird, 9, 21, 50, 65, 81, 86,
    92, 125
  as outsider, 79–80, 125
  Boo Radley and, 110–11
  trial of, 44, 51, 54, 58, 61–62, 63, 70,
    71, 72, 73, 74, 76, 84, 96–97, 100,
    101, 102, 105–9
"Romantic Regionalism of Harper
    Lee, The" (Erisman), 39–48
Ruark, Robert, 17–18

Sarton, May, 113
Scarlet Letter, The (Hawthorne), 76
Schuster, Edgar H., 7–15, 117
Scott, Walter, Sir, 39–40, 43
Scottsboro case, 68
"Secret Courts of Men's Hearts: Code
    and Law in Harper Lee's *To Kill a
    Mockingbird*, The" (Johnson),
    67–77
Selby, Keith, 116
Sexual taboo, 41
Shackelford, Dean, 115–25
Shakespeare, William, 1–2
Snow, symbolism of, 52, 100
Sound and the Fury, The (Faulkner), 55

South
  loss of insulation of, 46–48
  Maycomb as microcosm of, 40–43,
    53, 56–57, 59, 103
  romanticism of, 39–48
Steinbeck, John, 18
Stephanie, Miss, 21
"Store and Mockingbird: Two Pulitzer
    Novels about Alabama" (Going),
    61–66
Stowe, Harriet Beecher, 18, 57, 58
Stribling, T. S., 61
Sullivan, Richard, 64
Summertime boundaries, in *To Kill a
    Mockingbird*, 11, 12, 14
Superstition, in *To Kill a Mockingbird*,
    10, 11, 14–15, 21
Sykes, Reverend, 82, 94, 97

Tate, Alan, 105
Tate, Heck, 100, 113, 120
Tate, Sheriff, 54, 86
Taylor, Judge, 62
Taylor, W. R., 39
"Three at the Outset" (Hicks), 5
To Kill a Mockingbird, 5, 56–57, 58
  as autobiographical, 51–52, 68, 116,
    121
  censorship of, 23–38
  characters, 84–85
  Cry, the Beloved Country (Paton)
    versus, 17–22
  as Emersonian view of Southern
    Romanticism, 39–48
  emphatic positions in, 11–13
  equivocal moral resolutions in, 89–98
  female voice in, 115–25
  fusing of personal and social scenes
    in, 3–4
  historical context of, 68–69, 76–77,
    83–84
  human differences and, *see* Outsiders
  imagery and symbolism in, 86–87
  influences on, 57, 66
  intention and interpretation and,

13–14
language of, 82
law *versus* code in, 61–77, 80–81
as permanent work or period piece, 1–2
plot structure, 85–86
point of view in, 82
as regional novel, 39–48, 56–57
scale and, 8
as sentimentalized narrative, 93–94
setting, 83–84
structure and final synthesis and, 14–15
thematic motifs in, 9–11, 79–81
tone of, 82–83
tragic elements in, 49–58
universal themes in, 79–81
To Kill a Mockingbird (film), 117
childhood images in, 92–93, 116, 118
education in, 91
equivocal moral resolutions in, 89–98
female voice in, 115–25
Atticus Finch as main character in, 90, 116, 119, 121
Jem Finch in, 119
Scout Finch in, 116, 117–22, 125
gothic mode in, 95–96

lynch-mob and, 94–95
Maycomb and, 93, 117
mockingbird and, 91–92
Boo Radley and, 95–96
as sentimental narrative, 93–94
trial and, 93, 96–97, 116–17, 119
"voice-over" technique in, 90, 92, 118, 119–20
"*To Kill a Mockingbird:* Harper Lee's Tragic Vision" (Dave), 49–58
Tragedy, *To Kill a Mockingbird* as, 49–58
Twain, Mark, 18–19, 39, 43, 57

Uncle Tom's Cabin (Stowe), 57, 58
Underwood, Braxton, 21, 50, 8642

Warren, Robert Penn, 61
Welty, Eudora, 1, 3, 63
Wensley, Chris, 116
Whites, class distinctions among, 41–43
Whitman, Walt, 50–51
Woolf, Virginia, 53